FONS **TROMPENAARS**

DID THE
PEDESTRIAN DIE?

INSIGHTS FROM THE **GREATEST CULTURE GURU**

CAPSTONE

Copyright © Fons Trompenaars 2003

The right of Fons Trompenaars to be identified as the author of this work has been asserted in accordance with the Copyright, Designs and Patents Act 1988

First published 2003 by

Capstone Publishing Ltd (A John Wiley & Sons Co.)
8 Newtec Place
Magdalen Road
Oxford OX4 1RE
United Kingdom
http://www.capstoneideas.com

British Library Cataloguing in Publication Data

A CIP catalogue record for this book is available from the British Library

ISBN 1-84112-436-2

Typeset by
Forewords, 109 Oxford Road, Cowley, Oxford

Printed and bound by
T.J. International Ltd, Padstow, Cornwall

This book is printed on acid-free paper

Contents

Preface

Many readers who have seen and heard Fons Trompenaars at one of his conference presentations will immediately understand the title of this book: *Did the Pedestrian Die?*

At an early training workshop Fons asked the participants how they would respond to the dilemma which would arise if they happened to be a passenger in a car driven by a friend who then hit a pedestrian. Should they be concerned for the pedestrian or help their friend who would have to appear in court?

Fons has since posed this dilemma in international workshops and conferences across many different cultures, and also to some 65,000 managers captured in his cross-cultural database. Not only was the initial reaction different in different cultures, but the course of action the passenger would finally take, such as lying to protect their friend, was also dependent on the answer to the question "Did the pedestrian die?"

Whilst all could readily identify with the dilemma, this response was clearly culturally determined. A British person might feel more concerned to respect the law if the pedestrian died. A French person might feel more obligated to help their friend, arguing that friends are more important than unknown pedestrians.

This book is presented as a compilation of many such dilemmas that

Fons has identified and used to help both organizations and individual managers and leaders. Each element has been conceived, written, and then used all over the world; many were created after requests from clients, or developed from "moments of enlightenment" as Fons teased his research team or joked with fellow gurus. The individual contributions are on the one hand self-contained, but on the other hand form a whole that embraces the important issues facing the international leader and manager in today's ever-globalizing world. Together they provide a comprehensive digest of best practice and learning for modern business management.

University education and too much training are still failing today's generation of potential leaders and managers. These are still based on Cartesian logic and scientific method where problems are defined as closed systems and where the variables selected are those that can be measured and controlled. Apparently all we have to do is to evaluate alternate courses of action and select the one offering the lowest cost or highest margin. MBA students are still being taught to give sophisticated answers to the wrong type of question. Even in school laboratories pupils are told think in terms of keeping the temperature and pressure constant so they can study changes in volume. However, those who have to work in the real world know that a change in volume is not isothermal, but adiabatic: everything is connected to everything else. A problem is like surplus flab – tuck it in here, and it pops out somewhere else.

This book is different. It is an accumulation of a decade of researching cultural diversity and working across the globe with a wide range of organizations. Fons and his research team have been anxious to capture much of this tacit knowledge to identify the real issues and clarify what can really make a difference at the level of the individual and the organization as whole. In addition to his well-established cross-cultural database of managers from 65 countries across the world, Fons has "interviewed" thousands of business leaders and managers through a system based on interactive web pages. This WebCue system was originally conceived as a means to capture key issues from leaders and managers of client companies, often as preparation for future workshops or consultancy. These simulated interviews, following a semi-structured and open question format rather than simple multiple-choice questions, have been received with enormous enthusiasm by the business community. Here, at last, they can (often anonymously) formulate the actual issues and concerns they have in trying to grapple with real-world problems, tensions between competing priorities, demands, and values. Fons' new database of these responses is fascinating, but is now so large that a more rigorous means of analysis has been required to trawl the richness of these free-text, qualitative, value-laden responses. The aim is to elicit commonly recurring themes and define which issues are truly important and of real concern to the modern business leader and manager. The full spectrum of analytical software tools has been cast at this data.

The results of this analysis are consistent with experiences and feedback from conferences, workshops, and consulting assignments, showing that the wide spectrum of issues can be clustered into a number of categories of dilemmas, explored in this book.

Of particular interest is the consistency with which leaders and managers pose their problems as a series of extreme choices. These are typically issues like: Should we have the same products all over the world or should we have specialized products to meet local customer needs? Should we work in teams or as high-performing individuals? Should we send our technical expert to impress the client or our most senior member of staff, even though he knows little of the technology being offered? When evaluating these extreme choices or courses of action, we find they are either equally attractive or equally unattractive – but always apparently mutually exclusive.

In collaboration with Charles Hampden-Turner, Fons has created a new logic in which both goals can be achieved together, rather than one at the expense of the other. This process of dilemma reconciliation is demonstrated in the separate stories presented in this book. They represent the recurring dilemmas elicited from both the dilemma database, and observations and interventions from professional consulting best practice.

But that's not all. It would be a mistake to assume that operational level issues involve closed, solvable problems and that only the global challenges facing senior managers and leaders are characteristically open problems, manifesting themselves as dilemmas. The important lesson from this book is that if you listen carefully you will realize that all real-world problems are best considered as open problems and represented as dilemmas. Future leaders and managers will therefore benefit from changing their mindsets and viewing their challenges as open problems and expressing them as dilemmas. They can then begin to seek a reconciliation of the dilemmas, resulting in integrating seemingly opposing values. This results in the inclusion of a wider range of interests which would otherwise re-appear later.

Each element of this book is based on real business issues that are easy to recognize and relate to. Many are derived from client-led critical incidents. Some use parables or metaphors to illustrate both the elicitation of the dilemma and approaches to reconciliation. They are all worth reading; prepare to be stimulated and excited. Your satisfaction will come from knowing that at last someone understands the dilemmas you face every day.

Professor Peter Woolliams
Ashcroft International Business School
Anglia University, UK

CHAPTER 1

Did the pedestrian die?

Many of the elements in *Did The Pedestrian Die?* try to provide an alternative to the linear thinking of both professionals in the field of cross-cultural management and typical MBA students. When discussing how different cultures respond to the dilemma they face as a passenger after a car accident, participants at workshops often laugh at the different responses, especially when I comment that in France friends are more important than pedestrians. Laughter – as a result of humor – is very important in the work of my organization. Arthur Koestler described the essence of humor as two very opposite logics suddenly turning out to be both equally logical. And, that in, turn spotlights something common to all humanity. We all share the same dilemmas but our culture makes one horn of the dilemma more dominant than the other. I have often asked audiences in Asia, North America, Africa and Europe if they would be comfortable being in a situation in which their friends might need them to lie for them. I haven't had one single participant who seemed to like it. Dilemmas are universal, it seems, while the answers are culturally determined.

SO – *DID* THE PEDESTRIAN DIE?

You are a passenger in a car driven by a close friend. He hits a pedestrian. You know he was going at least 35 miles per hour in an area of the city where the maximum speed allowed is 20 miles per hour. There are no witnesses. His lawyer says that if you are prepared to testify under oath that he was only driving at 20 miles per hour it may save him from serious consequences.

What right has your friend to expect you to protect him?

(a) My friend has a *definite* right, as a friend, to expect me to testify to the lower figure.

(b) He has *some* right, as a friend, to expect me to testify to the lower figure.

(c) He has *no* right, even as a friend, to expect me to testify to the lower figure.

Would you help your friend in view of the obligations you feel towards society?

(d) I would testify to the lower figure.

(e) I would not testify to the lower figure.

This dilemma has been put to some 65,000 managers in 65 countries. Obviously one would expect the answers to vary considerably from country to country, and they do. In Switzerland and North America more than 93 percent chose the combination (c) and (e), while in China and Venezuela less than 35 percent showed a preference for this answer. The results completely align with expectations in the international business world where reliability and integrity are at stake. The Germans, Dutch, British, and Americans are seen as reliable and knowing how to behave in an ethically correct manner. They are therefore considered more reliable than Asians and South Americans, who always help their friends, and seem not to be bothered – in or out of business – by ethical principles. Nothing new here.

The interpretation of these results in the previous paragraph is obviously culturally biased. Consider the following remark from a Korean who came to me during a break in a workshop and said "I knew Americans were corrupt but you gave it empirical evidence, thank you." I asked how. "You can't trust the Americans, they don't even help their friends," he answered.

I have posed the car accident question to a large variety of people and I have never met anyone who would like to experience the actual situation. This type of dilemma is beyond culture. It is seen as a dilemma in all societies because everybody, regardless of their culture, would like to help their friends as well as respect the truth and support the laws that protect pedestrians. Culture is the way one solves dilemmas; that is, the way one resolves dilemmas is culturally determined.

Talcott Parsons, in his book *The Social System*, referred to the underlying issue as the difference between Universalism and Particularism. The first is a value orientation popular in Protestant societies. Here order and authority prevail, codified in writing and checked by God and lawyers. On the other side of the spectrum we find Particularism, popular amongst Catholics, who seem to be rather charmed by the exception: God wasn't looking during the accident and a feeling of guilt is often ridiculed. In Universalistic countries there is often a need to look for standards (the hotel chain, ISO, Basic

Business Principles, McDonald's, Coca-Cola). In Particularistic countries the exceptional and the unique are more popular (Le Chateau, Haute Cuisine, or Haute Couture).

International organizations are increasingly confronted with these types of value dilemmas. They are easy to solve in those multinationals in which Italians work in Italy and Americans work in the USA. You just allow for different approaches in different cultures. It becomes more troublesome when the process of internationalization develops further. The quest for Business Principles in global organizations increases in order to enable the organization to superimpose a common set of ethical values.

Consider the following multinational American organization that espouses two Business Principles: Uncompromising Integrity and Respect for Diversity. After I had confronted its senior employees with the car accident dilemma, I asked them how they would approach this dilemma in practice when integrity was their leading value. A variety of answers drew my attention. The Chinese and Italians would lie for their friends (the unique part of any relationship) whereas the English, Dutch, and North Americans put the law (the universal truth) above anything. The introduction of the second principle, Respect for Diversity, made the consistent application of integrity even more complex than it was initially.

In Universalistic cultures, the concept of integrity is often seen as a "garbage can" concept of what is allowed in one's own environment and which is laid down in law. In dominant ones, such as the US and Germany, integrity is nothing more than a natural extension of their own cultures. I was presenting the pedestrian dilemma to an international group of managers. An Englishman confessed that he would give his friend some right to expect him to lie but it could have easily been a definite right or no right at all. In an attempt to be amusing I then added that the pedestrian was very dead. "But why didn't you give us this information at the beginning?" asked a Frenchwoman, with great irritation. "Why should I?" was my reply, "what's your problem?" "Like my English colleague my answer was 'b', some right," she answered. "But now that I know that my friend has killed a pedestrian, I realize I should have answered 'a': he has a definite right to expect my help." The critical fact here was the pedestrian's state of health, and you should have seen the face of the Englishman! It confirmed that in France friends are more important than pedestrians, and if you know the streets of Paris, you will know what I mean.

Last year I was invited to participate in a conference dealing with Business Ethics. The goal of the conference was to publish the result of large-scale research in a number of European countries. One of the questions was: If you have signed a contract, would you have to stick to it in all circumstances? The answers had to be given on a five-point scale ranging from always to never. An interesting question. However, the research was sponsored solely by the Dutch and the results and their interpretation were unfortunately, therefore, very predictably seen from a Dutch perspective. Italians, for example, scored at the lowest end of the scale of ethical behavior (if they answered truthfully) and the Germans at the highest. For the Italians it was not always ethical to adhere to a contract under circumstances that demanded a flexible approach. In contrast, it seemed that the Germans expected a contract to be fulfilled even if one of the parties involved suffered as a result. In fact, the methodology adopted in this research measured how Dutch the sponsors were rather than highlighting the differing ethical behavior of the participants.

The international manager needs a new logic. And research on international ethics needs to be undertaken by an international team. The logic should be based on the etymological meaning of the word integrity: unaffected condition, in a completely integrated whole. Once one goes international one needs this new logic in order to survive. Based on the cumulative evidence we have collected, I strongly believe that the international understanding of the concept of integrity should be the result of integrating seemingly opposing values.

A Japanese workshop participant came to me in a break. He said that in Japan he would test the strength of his friendship by asking his friend to tell the truth in court. In the meantime, he would go to the judge and plead for a lower sentence on the grounds of his friend's courage and bad luck. Here integrity deals with the question of how to reconcile the particular friendship with the universal truth. This integration makes it into a virgin unity – and no culture will object to that.

CITATIONS, CERTAINTIES AND CHANGE

Our western business education has given ample food to the denial of any dilemmas in business. These are not what they teach in business education. Reality is put on a line and, depending on the circumstances, you choose the most effective position on that line.

Geert Hofstede is the most cited social scientist in the Netherlands. Over the years he has built up an international reputation with his work in the field of intercultural management. A justified reputation? Absolutely. If you are frequently cited, then you certainly have something exceptional to say. But how is this defined? A list of how often people are cited only shows how often scientists are quoted by other scientists. They are of importance to the academic world; after all, an essential part of writing an academic article is to cite your sources.

The fact that, in academia, so many references are made to the work of Hofstede reveals more about the state of that world than it does about the groundbreaking work Hofstede has carried out with his thirty-year-old material. Many others, including myself, who focus on forming theory around intercultural management, owe a lot to his work. Charles Hampden-Turner and I even used his dimensions and insights in our book *Riding the Waves of Culture* in order to describe the differences in orientation between cultures.

Given such a promising start, it is a pity that during the past thirty years Hofstede has hardly added anything at all to his model – no method of reconciling differences, for example. Pioneers are often proclaimers rather than acclaimers. So far so good. However, Hofstede's approach has several serious limitations. Here also we see that business reality and culture are mapped as positions on a line.

Firstly, look at the arbitrary way in which Hofstede has chosen five dimensions to describe culture. He applied statistical methods to data obtained from different social research surveys within IBM (where he originally worked). These statistical methods were not developed to map cultural differences. Four dimensions appeared, followed later by a fifth. The danger here is that a number of dimensions are forgotten because they happen not to have been researched.

Hofstede does not, for example, mention important dimensions such as the degree to which emotions are shown and the perception of self-control over your environment (compare judo and boxing, whereby the former involves using the strength of your opponent to your advantage) and the depth of relationships (from specific to diffuse). Such inductive research methodology always has its limitations; we cannot completely map the human race.

The second objection is that Hofstede's model is notably ethnocentric. Questions asked are not only dated, but really only measure how the Dutch would reduce uncertainty or how they would define a feminine person.

Thirdly, a linear approach has a number of serious limitations. I remember the time when Charles Hampden-Turner reacted to my thesis with a worried look: "Oh my God, another Dutchman using simplistic, mutually exclusive categories." Only ten years later did I understand the depth of his question as to why an individualist would not be able to contribute to a collectivity and why successful people do not take risks in certain areas of their lives in order to be able to look other uncertainties full in the face. Hampden-Turner pointed out the greatest shortcomings in the approach of most Western scientists.

Hofstede also places values on a straight scale, the ends of which exclude each other. It is precisely in the linking of opposite values that essential meaning becomes apparent. Further analysis reveals that those cultures in which individual creativity is at the disposal of the wider community create the most wealth. In the same way, communities that learn through exceptions to improve rules, as well as those that integrate masculine and feminine values, are superior to cultures that see values as mutually exclusive artifacts. Unfortunately for Hofstede, but especially for his followers, this will negatively determine the success of the social sciences in the future, as it presents an impoverished view of reality.

As far as methodology is concerned, the field of intercultural management seems to be stranded on this superficial approach, which at first sight appears so attractive. To be able to position the world in two-by-two matrices is wonderful – moreover, it is the preferred approach of many other consultants.

The fourth objection concerns the applicability of Hofstede's approach. During the period when I too used the same methods in my advisory practice, it quickly became apparent that our large database was often used to lend empirical weight to cultural stereotypes, which were mainly negative. Rather than saying "typically German," we say that it is "typical uncertainty avoidance behavior combined with low power distance." Table 1.1 summarizes the assumptions of Hofstede versus those of Trompenaars/Hampden-Turner.

It is time that interculturalists, who are so essential to the current globalization and integration of merger and take-over processes, develop themselves in the area of what we can call "transcultural management." This approach makes grateful use of models, but goes a number of steps further. For practical purposes, people experience a need to add depth to the scientific insight that the models afford. Based on the evidence of research, I believe that culture as well as business processes are cybernetic systems in need of feedback. And since I approach culture and business as cybernetic systems it becomes crucial that there are well-established feedback loops enabling these systems to learn.

Table 1.1

Hofstede assumes:	Trompenaars and Hampden-Turner assume:
• Cultures are static points on dual axis maps.	• Cultures dance from one preferred end to the opposite, and back.
• One cultural category excludes its opposite.	• One cultural category seeks to "manage" its opposite.
• "Independent" factors account for "dependent" variables.	• Value dimensions self-organize in systems to generate new meanings.
• Established statistical procedures are culture neutral and value free.	• Established statistical procedures are ulturally biased and value full.
• Cultures are linear with "more" or "less" of a fixed quality.	• Cultures are circles with preferred arcs joined together.
• Data derived from IBM are superior to ideas drawn from academic research and reflect management's convictions.	• Data derived from IBM are but pale imitations of academic research and reflect management's compliance.
• Hofstede, by thinking inductively, derived his categories from IBM data and originated his own scales.	• Hofstede, by thinking inductively, reinvented the scales from which IBM had plagiarized their questions.
• There is no better place to be on the quadrant maps and no answer to the questions "so what?" and "where should we move?"	• There is no better place to start on the seven dimensions, but moves to integrate and reconcile values lead to superior performance.

Finally, anticipating what is probably coming…

• A priori concepts like "dilemma" are metaphysical constructs with no basis in empirical research and with no testable validity or means of verification.	• Dilemma has been part of culture from Classic Greek Tragedy and the Primordial Opposites of the Tao, through Shakespeare to the binary codes of anthropologists today.
• All cultures are different although those differences can be expressed as positions of relative salience on four variables.	• All cultures are similar in the dilemmas they confront, yet different in the solutions they find, which transcend the opposites creatively.

Hofstede took the all-important first step. However, we can accuse the social scientists of still clinging to his outdated method. Hofstede should count himself lucky if he is still the most quoted scientist in the Netherlands in five years' time. Especially since he is quoted mainly by those who criticize him and suggest alternatives – something which is absolutely necessary.

MEDIOCRE BUT ARROGANT

What is the only reason for a company to centralize and decentralize? This is a question I like to ask MBA students attending my lectures on International Management. Without hesitation, slogans like flexibility, control, and the need to standardize will be voiced. I ask the students to think first which, very often, is not what they learn to do with an MBA education. After a period of silence, I whisper to them that the only reason for an organization to centralize is the extent to which it is decentralized. The smart MBAs understand quickly that this also holds true for decentralization. MBA students are very often encouraged to give simple answers of uni-dimensional nature to very complex processes – "if this, then that" – based upon competing logics that exclude each other.

By comparison with the legal profession, there are fewer jokes made about people with MBAs. Despite that, this large group of monomanic educated people can in the long run threaten our civilization, and not only the business world. Why are people with an MBA not kept out of harm's way? And even worse, the title is displayed on business cards with pride. Of course the advocates of this type of business education will refer to the many MBAs who are responsible for the Anglo-Saxon economic success formula, like the recipes developed by business schools: Emotional Intelligence, Reengineering, Core Competence, Stick to the Knitting, Shareholder Value…When people are called "human resources" it will not hurt if you stab them in the back. Every two years, one superficial, over-hyped theory is replaced by another.

The last one-dimensional invention, of which we must feel ashamed, is Shareholder Value. Together with Kees Storm of AEGON and Jaap Vink of CSM, I have never understood what is so wonderful about this. First of all, it is only these shareholders who have no idea of the meaning of "sharing." I re-read the book *One-dimensional Man* by Marcuse, and I think it is time for the One-dimensional Organization. The conclusions are again poor. Don't get me wrong: I am not against Shareholder Value. But there are other orientations whereby values like Employer Value, Consumer Value, and Societal Value can be integrated. Wealth is created in the tension between these orientations. The Stakeholder model must come back again, but shareholders say "Isn't it true that recent economic development is based on the fact that we go for more profit, the support of the shareholders? We have never before created so many jobs, we have got rid of the financial deficit, we have enabled a new economy. All of this is created by shareholder value."

And yet people cannot apply a simple, single-sighted approach to justify the mechanism of a complex process. Value is created through combining a company's interest with that of the other parties. Long-term vision is needed here, which is very often the unknown factor for Anglo-Saxon shareholders. "Going for the next buck," "the one-minute manager," and "You're only as good as your last performance" are familiar statements. Kees Storm told me in an interview that he never understood the contradiction between shareholder value and stakeholder value. According to him, customers create value. "Our first job is to satisfy our customers. This can only be achieved by motivated employees who have access to the capital market. This is of crucial importance for Aegon, and it can only be done by sufficiently rewarding investors."

It is the leader's responsibility to bring the parties involved together and to find the right balance. If one of the stakeholders has the upper hand, this will create a vicious circle. Vink once mentioned to me that it is difficult to discuss anything other than shareholder value with financial analysts, which is logical. It has to do with young, bright MBAs who are described as visionary when looking further than the next quarter.

These are the reasons why French and German politicians worry about the "hostile takeover" developed in the Anglo-Saxon world. It is based purely on technical one-dimensional thinking and seldom leaves other aspects intact. In the past I have indicated that this will unavoidably lead to value destruction. Luckily, we can see that the integration of values occurs naturally by offering young employees stock options, especially if the value of the options increases in the long-term (five years). Shareholder value is equal to stakeholder value if we give it a five-year time-span. I think we have to wait until Wall Street crashes (hopefully in a small way): Then the MBAs will again assume the position that they should always have held, thinking hard, being full of doubts – and also being far removed from any situation in which they brilliantly answer fundamentally wrong questions.

THE TOUGH CONSEQUENCES OF A LACK OF FEEDBACK

The consequences of the terrorist attacks on New York and Washington in September 2001, especially after the retaliation in Afghanistan, have manifested themselves in our purse and in a perceived lack of security: feelings that have been prevalent for a long time outside the Western world. Now this is not meant as an excuse for terrorism of any sort; on the contrary, no form of terrorism is ever acceptable.

However, we should ask how it is possible that a group of terrorists is able to develop such a strongly felt hatred that its members are willing to give up their lives. How can a malignant tumor spread to such an extent? These are legitimate questions, as is the question of how international business can contribute to the resolution of the dilemmas facing today's citizens.

What are these dilemmas? There are many, but three of them are particularly salient and terrifying.

We can formulate the first dilemma as on the one hand we need to fight any form of terrorism, while on the other hand we need to fight the root causes of the underlying hatred. This is a version of the well-known short-term paradigm of shooting from the hip, versus the long-term belief that we have to accept a certain number of casualties in the name of the patience that will kill the roots of evil. There is no halfway house; both need to be integrated. The events of 11 September caused the short-term pain to be severely felt. It can also be seen in other – related – areas: for example, how can we avoid the vicious circle that Arafat and Sharon have created? The only long-term thinking that we can see in these two leaders is their mutual intimacy with the past.

Bush also reacted emotionally and couldn't see beyond the short-term. I think we owe it to Colin Powell that we now have a chance of tackling the roots of the problem. Could we perhaps replace short-sighted retaliation at unknown targets, sponsored by a US$40 billion anti-terrorism budget, with a decrease in the debt of third world countries? And could not part of this immense budget be dedicated to increasing the appallingly low incomes that Western companies seem to pay to labor in countries like Indonesia or Pakistan? Here one can see a role for business to play. After mutual agreement, increased stable production could be repaid with peace...

A second dilemma has to do with the fact that on the one hand terrorism jeopardizes the whole world, while on the other hand it can be seen as a weapon of last resort for the poor, a way of telling the world that they're still here. All societies that are based on trust are used to discussing problems with unhappy people before they turn to murder. But will we still be able to see a Muslim without thinking that he or she is covered with explosives? Every airplane has become a potential bomb and every skyscraper a tomb. Obviously we have to fight terrorism, but only in a world where the state has a monopoly on fighting and where that fighting is kept under the stringent control of governments. In a world without global laws we have to give this authority to a superpower. If not to the United Nations, then we should give it to the US, the only state that has the power to use it. However, things need to happen in a world where the weak have a vote, then they will have no more need for the terror that leads to increased poverty and hatred. Business needs to take this responsibility in places where the dilemma reveals itself within its own organizations. Listening to people distant from head offices might be a good start. Also, signals picked up at head offices could help increase the quality of the rules and policies that radiate out to their satellites.

Finally, there is the dilemma between the ultimate evil of the attack on the World Trade Center and the consequences of the foreign politics of the United States. Any suicide attacks – where the guilty cannot receive any feedback about the consequences of their actions – are an example of ultimate evil. This is a vicious circle in which mass murder and self-destruction are signals of a breakdown in communications, creating a downward spiral. It is an example of an unreconciled dilemma, with caution and courage translated into cowardice and recklessness. This stands in great contrast to the courage displayed by the heroes of the New York Fire Department who reconciled caution and courage to save thousands of people. We can define a few causes of this dilemma. For quite some time now it has been possible to describe American foreign policy as naïve, causing unintended consequences that led to the recent tragedy. You cannot, for example, provide unconditional support to the Israeli state without frequently checking the reasonableness of its actions.

This seems like a metaphor for the policies of many large American multinationals. Time and again their executives try to superimpose a certain Anglo-Saxon way of thinking – supported by a MBA, the Coca-Cola of business education. The pathology of both terrorism and an insensitive globalism (American or European) can be traced back to a system that lacks feedback. Like terrorists, some multinationals have made themselves insensitive to feedback, leading to self-destruction. The business world should attempt to break the vicious circle of universalistic globalization at the cost of local sensitivities. We have seen some exemplary (American) organizations that use local insights and learning to increase the quality of their global offering.

FROM BALANCE TO WORK/LIFE INTEGRATION

It have noticed that I develop a feeling of stress only when I have problems at home, and this feeling overwhelms me when I am on the brink on leaving for vacation. Can I openly take my laptop along or do I have to smuggle it ? How many books can go in the suitcase? OK, I promise not to answer any emails.

It is beyond doubt that every active person in the world feels a tension between their work and their private life. You just need to look up the concept of work/life balance on the Internet search engine Google and you will get more than 83,000 hits. The problem starts with the expression itself: work/life balance. Because we speak of a balance we seem to suppose that when the work is tilted uppermost, it is at the cost of private life and vice versa. Moreover it seems that work is done outside the sphere of life: interesting. It is in these very assumptions that a large part of the problem is created. As a consequence we can understand why many of the proposed solutions to this subject manifest themselves as the provision of nursery facilities, fitness programs and corporate outings. Actually these are only compromise offerings. Work/life balance has to be extended to work/life integration to resolve the true problem.

A brief look at the essential literature shows how complex this subject is. It is summarized in five overlapping models. We can also see how much they are affected by cultural differences.

The first is the *segmentation* model in which it is assumed that work and activities outside of work are completely separate and that they do not influence each other. In predominantly specific cultures, one expects private problems not to be discussed at work, and that at home the saying "no shop talk" dominates. Then there is the *spillover* model in which one assumes that both spheres of life can influence each other. A third model, *compensation,* suggests that what one lacks at work is compensated for in private life, and vice versa. For example, if you do a lot of routine work without too many challenges, you would be inclined to become an overactive director of a football or social club in your spare time from which you could derive more satisfaction. Then there is the *instrumental* model in which success in one sphere of life helps achievements in the other. For example, in diffuse cultures such as those of Southern Europe, you can use the status you gain at work to get an extra discount in the purchase of a car. Finally, there is the *conflict* model. Here one assumes that the ever-increasing demands in all spheres of life force people to make choices. So you are allowed to work very hard and in an extremely responsible role, as long as you know that dinner starts at six every evening.

All these models are implicitly a consequence of the "border theory" developed by Sue Campbell Clark. This assumes that people cross borders every day but in different ways. On the basis of this assumption we will never find a creative reconciliation for the dilemma between our working and our non-working life. In particular, and at levels of senior leadership, we can only find long term solutions when we depart from the imaginary line connecting "life" and "work."

We therefore need a new sixth model that I will call the *integration* model. Dilemmas of this nature can only be resolved if work helps you to raise the quality of other life spheres, and when non-work related activities can help you enrich work. Here again the dynamics between the culture of the family and the culture of the organization determine the nature of the dilemma and the way it is approached. In this context the typical Anglo-Saxon notion of "quality time" is a good example of reconciliation. However, it is used in that culture as a way to selectively go deeply into your private life while not being disturbed by work-related matters. The reconciliation of a series of few precious moments is used in a European context to apply essential lessons of life while at work. It achieves the same reconciliation in the end, but the start and end points are reversed. In many Asian and Latin cultures in which family is central, we clearly see a natural reconciliation of work and private life in their numerous family businesses. The most intimate private problems are collectively discussed at work, and home is an important haven where the most crucial strategic businesses are resolved.

Jewish culture recognizes the "Sabbatical" which was not intended to allow for a rest period but, as in the original meaning of Sabbath, as a way to enhance future research by new information and a period of reflection. In this way we have the notion of the vacation in Europe, so much ignored by North Americans. In a healthy society, a vacation is used to accumulate energy in a peaceful and relaxed private setting in order to increase your effectiveness at work when your return. You can, of course, exaggerate as in Germany, where people seem to argue that work takes up too much free time, or as in Japan and America, where people seem to work so hard that heart attacks and suicides are unexceptional. But one can also find that colleagues can be extemely useful (by being removed) as a resource for solving private problems. In my own business life I have never taken a single strategic decision before listening to my wife's advice. Just call it integration.

CHAPTER 2

Leadership: reconciling the dilemmas of today

As a leader you have to inspire as well as listen. You have to make decisions yourself but also delegate, and you need to centralize your organization around local responsibilities. As a professional, you need to master your materials and at the same time you need to be passionately at one with the mission of the whole organization. You need to apply your brilliant analytic skills in order to place these contributions in a larger context. You are supposed to have priorities and put them in a meticulous sequence, while parallel processing is in vogue. You have to develop a brilliant strategy and at the same time have all the answers to questions in case your strategy misses its goals. Phew! No wonder there are so many definitions of effective leadership.

There is a need for a new paradigm, for the development of a meta-theory of leadership that transcends culture. This is again based on the same logic that pervades this book. Research reveals clearly that competence in reconciling dilemmas is the most discriminating feature that differentiates successful and less successful leaders. Leaders increasingly need to "manage culture" by – very carefully – fine-tuning dilemmas. This also means, increasingly, that the culture leads the organization. The leader defines what an organization views as excellent and develops an appropriate culture, thereby ensuring that the organization cannot do anything other than excel.

ENTERING THE 21ST CENTURY AS A MANAGER OR A LEADER?

You just need to open the newspapers to be faced with a variety of descriptions of successful leaders. During the first round of the 2002 French presidential election, the *Financial Times* outlined the fact that Chirac had surpassed Jospin in the popularity polls for the first time, ascribing this to the fact that his highly affectionate relationship with his grandson was helping to promote him as a real father figure. Chirac was seen as "sympa, génial et approachable."

A while back *De Volkskrant*, a quality Dutch newspaper, reported that entrepreneurs were not "sympa" at all, they were contrary machos who dared to fail. In the same newspaper the American columnist Michael Lewis declared that American entrepreneurs distinguished themselves by having unshakeable faith in their own ideas. European entrepreneurs prefer to play it safe, as Nina Brink showed when she sold WorldonLine to naïve Dutch investors and the internationally-known rich, like Mick Jagger and Tina Turner, for 400 percent of its real worth.

A quick scan through the literature on leadership reveals striking differences over time as well as between French, American, and Japanese authors. That is understandable. To be successful in France you need to be part of the right network, have the right education, and possess a certain amount of charisma. In Japan, being male, possessing seniority, and the right education (yes, even going to the right kindergarten) helps; wisdom certainly does no harm. In the US having a touch of vision, mission, and some Business Principles would suffice. But what makes a good leader in an international context?

My organization – Trompenaars Hampden-Turner – has looked into this recently by interviewing thousands of leaders and asking them the following question:

Take these descriptions of a good manager. Which one would you choose?

(a)   Good leaders are people who continuously help their subordinates to solve the variety of problems that they face. They are like parents, not teachers.

(b)   Good leaders occupy a position between that of a private coach and a teacher. Their effectiveness depends on how they balance both roles.

(c)   Good leaders get things done. They set goals, give information, measure results and let people do their own work in that context

(d)   Good leaders give a lot of attention to work streams, so that goals, tasks and achievements are aimed at improving those processes.

(e)   Good leaders get things done. They set goals, give information and measure results so that everyone is embedded in continuous work streams.

I gave this question to several top leaders. I was not surprised by the fact that leaders such as Richard Branson of Virgin, Michael Dell of Dell Computers, Kees Storm of AEGON, and Laurent Beaudoin of Bombardier made significantly different choices from people on our database of more "ordinary" managers. Do you know what the difference was?

The leaders described in answer "a" look like those of the beginning of the last century: Listen to father and everything will be OK. This style is still very popular in Latin America and Asia, where we have also conducted the research, compared to Europe and the US. There is nothing wrong with that, but it is quite limited in its applicability outside these regions. Answer "b" is a typical compromise and will not work very well anywhere. Answer "c" is very popular amongst Anglo-Saxons and North-West European managers. The ever-popular "Management by Objectives" is again applied recklessly. Add some vision and mission, and you're the modern leader; but the French would quickly argue: "Whose vision and mission is it?" Answers "d" and "e" are two alternative ways to integrate seemingly opposing values on a higher level and would therefore have my approval. Answer "d" suggests that good leaders guide people who make mistakes and learn from them, while "e" integrates the dichotomy of task orientation with work streams in the opposite direction. The last two choices were made much more frequently by more successful leaders. Why all the fuzz?

Recent studies on leadership by Warren Bennis and John Kotter have tried to capture certain finite characteristics of good leadership. In typical American fashion they have listed four universal characteristics of effective leadership: attention, trust, self-knowledge, and meaningfulness. Other Anglo-Saxons have come up with alternative lists. If you read the French book *Les Grand Patrons*, by Christine Ockrent and Jean Pierre Séréni, you will find a completely different view of what makes leaders effective. This causes a great deal of confusion for the trans-cultural manager. If the French manage in France, the Japanese in Japan, and the Americans in the US there is no problem. But increasingly you find that leaders have to deal with multicultural groups. Which paradigm should they follow? Which meaning should they create? Which principles should they follow if they need to act in a multicultural setting? This is where the need for a meta-theory of leadership, transcending culture, is most clearly seen.

LEADERSHIP DILEMMAS

Managers very often have to cope with problems they need to solve; leaders are continuously dealing with dilemmas that they need to reconcile on a higher level. It goes without saying that managers often can't sleep, because they don't achieve their goals, while this happens to leaders only when they can't reconcile a number of conflicting objectives. It is difficult enough to complete a job; however, it is even harder if you don't know which job to complete. Even worse, integrating seemingly opposing values often leads to a new dilemma. It is a continuous process.

What kind of dilemmas do leaders face? After interviewing many leaders it appears that the following are those which most frequently occur.

Dilemma 1: standard and adaptation. It is remarkable how often leaders mentioned this dilemma. Do we have to globalize our approach or do we just have to localize? Is it more beneficial for our organization to choose mass production than focus on specialized products? Effective leaders found the solution in the "transnational organization" where best local practices are globalized on a continuous basis. "Mass customization" is the keyword for reconciling standardized production and specialized adaptations.

Dilemma 2: individual creativity and team spirit. A second leadership dilemma is the integration of team spirit with individual creativity and a competitive mindset. The effective leader knows how to make an excellent team out of creative individuals. The team is stimulated to support brilliant individuals, while these individuals deploy themselves for the greater whole. This has been called co-opetition.

Dilemma 3: passion and control. Is a good leader an emotional and passionate person or does the control of emotions make a better leader? Here there are two clear types. Passionate leaders without reason are neurotics, and neutral leaders without emotions are robots. Richard Branson regularly checks his passion with reason, and if we look at the more neutral Jack Welch, the former CEO of General Electric, we see a leader who gives his controlled reason meaning by showing passion once in a while.

Dilemma 4: Analysis and synthesis. Is the leader of the 21st century a detached, analytical person who is able to divide the big picture into ready-to-eat pieces, always selecting for shareholder value? Or is it somebody who puts issues in the big picture and gives priority to the rather vaguely defined stakeholder value? At Shell, Van Lennep's "helicopter view" was introduced as a significant characteristic of a modern leader – the capability to ascend and keep the overview, while being able to zoom in on certain aspects of the matter. Jan Carlzon (SAS) called the integration of specific moments with profundity, as a part of client service, "moments of truth." This is another significant characteristic of the modern leader, namely the ability to know when and where to go in deep. Pure analysis leads to paralysis, and the overuse of synthesis leads to an infinite holism and a lack of action.

Dilemma 5: doing and being. "Getting things done" is an important characteristic of a manager. However, shouldn't we keep the rather vulgar "doing" in balance with "being," as in our private lives? As a leader you have to be yourself as well. From our research it appeared that successful leaders act the way they really are. They seem to be one with the business they are undertaking. One of the important causes of stress is that "doing" and "being" are not integrated. Excessive compulsion to perform, when not matching an individual's true personality, leads to ineffective behavior.

Dilemma 6: Sequential and parallel. Notably, effective leaders are able to plan in a rigorous sequential way, but at the same time have the ability to stimulate parallel processes. This reconciliation, which we know as "synchronize processes to increase the sequential speed" – or "Just In Time" management – seems also to be very effective in integrating the long and short term.

Dilemma 7: push and pull. This final core competence for today's leaders is the ability to connect the voice of the market with the technology the company has developed and vice versa. This is not about technology push or market pull. The modern leader knows that the push of technology finally leads to the ultimate niche market, that part without any clients. If you only choose for the market, your clients will be unsatisfied. I believe that leaders are not adding value, because only simple values add up. Values are combined by leaders; a car which is both fast and safe, high-quality food which is also easy to prepare. Nobody claims that combining values is easy; nevertheless, it is possible. A computer that is capable of making extremely complex calculations can also be user friendly. The ever-expanding system of satisfaction of values will form the ultimate test for the leaders of this century.

THE PRACTICAL SIDE OF MULTICULTURAL MANAGEMENT

This month I was invited by a large, internationally operating consulting firm to comment at their international partner conference on the multicultural challenges experienced by many of their impressive clients. The purpose was to engage a discussion between their consultants and those in the field. Normally, clients are not so keen to share their deeper insights in such an environment, and consultants are even more polite than usual in order not to embarrass their clients. So I was pleasantly surprised by the relevant issues they raised. A variety of senior managers from the automotive, pharmaceutical, consulting, and chemical industries each gave a ten-minute introduction. Their individual stories only gave a glance at the true problems an organization faces when going into multicultural environments. However, adding up their experiences looks like the beginnings of a handbook for coping with the challenges of getting international. Drawing on their experience in conducting business in a multicultural environment, the speakers presented certain business principles and methodologies that they believed effectively dealt with the challenges they faced in becoming successful internationally. Let me sum up the collective findings.

Understand cultural differences. In order to bridge the cultural gap and harmonize cultural differences, you first need to recognize and become aware of those cultural differences. Behavior, norms, values, notions of relationships, time and space, and even the concepts of commitment and expectation, are all culturally determined. Differences between business operations in different cultures should be understood as a first step toward understanding conflicting behavior. Representatives of both the pharmaceutical and automotive industries (loaded with merger and acquisitions experience) said their organizations had taken serious attempts to look at the differences. But they did it in their own particular way. One CFO stated that stakeholders were increasingly taking into account the values embedded in companies:

> Companies are becoming more socially aware. After the merger we sat all the CFOs down round a table, and we got into mixed pairs. We then got all the issues out and confronted them as soon as possible. We asked senior managers to be open about what they thought were the best and worse practices in both organisations. We got positives and negatives on the table as soon as possible in order to become aware of each other's perceptions of mutual practices. It was an eye-opener and this communication was a head start in understanding our cultural differences.

A senior partner of the consulting firm concluded. "Multicultural relationships must be managed in the global business environment," he said. "Business should be conducted based on a value system in order to deal effectively with the challenges presented in a multicultural environment."

Respect different cultures. Cultural differences should be respected if harmony and synergies are to be established in a multicultural environment. In order to develop respect, everyone agreed that it was crucial to attain a common value framework for the diversity of cultures. For most organizations present, people were engaged in co-defining shared corporate core values within which obvious differences were allowed.

In this process, it is important that management is consistent, living its own values and standards, both from a personal and a business ethics point of view. This behavior starts with really living what is said and fulfilling any promises made, thereby establishing trust. Account should be taken of different cultures in a global organization. A global corporate culture should be firm but flexible. In order to establish respect for cultural differences, it is of utmost importance that we do not only look at the differences but also at common factors. One organization took a much harder position, because of the personality of its CEO: Only after business issues were harmonized and business processes were rationalized was attention given to the value side of the integration. It did have a troublesome beginning, though it now seems to work quite well.

A culturally diverse team needs to be seen as an asset rather than as a liability. The broader "bandwidth" of experience and combined frame of reference leads to better quality decision making. It is of course important that the cultural differences in the team are harmonized and that the team's common goals and visions are shared and bought into by the whole team.

Building trust between members of multicultural teams. Establishing and respecting trust is a cornerstone for strong multicultural relationships, and personal involvement is important to establish and strengthen these. Building trust comes from genuine involvement and commitment, but that trust does not come quickly or easily. Investing in building relationships with key individuals is critical in a multicultural environment.

The morality and ethics of the different cultures involved should be understood. It is important to get alignment and agreement in applying the morality and values of yourself and your company in different cultural environments. Key, in this context, is defining a shared purpose and shared aspirations, always following through what you say you are going to do with actions, and never doing anything that undermines your integrity. The introduction of a value-based framework can be very helpful, providing it is one which does not attempt to bring people who think differently in to line, but rather attempts to find common values and shared aspirations to use as a base. In situations where managers are confronted by "gray areas" or have to compromise on culture in order to progress a transaction or issue, it is still important to set goals and act to achieve these within the framework of a value system.

Reconciliation. A further step in achieving cultural harmony lies in reconciling the different cultures. This involves the understanding of differences, and also flexibility and adaptation to change by these different cultures, without compromising values and beliefs.

Other principles of importance are to ensure that there are no losers when conducting business in a multicultural environment, but that a win–win situation is always achieved. "Getting down to work and getting projects done is important in getting a merged company functioning," commented one of the senior leaders. Also, transferring staff between merged companies can be a very effective multicultural tool.

It is encouraging to see these comments being made by ordinary business managers, not only because of what they say, but also because of why they say these things. The level of understanding and the level of respect they have shown by not just going for the "My Way" solution has definitely provided them with the benefit of avoiding a lot of unnecessary frustration and misunderstanding. It also ultimately brings a much richer common solution.

MICHAEL DELL'S EARLY DISCOVERIES

At the beginning of May 1996 my office received a phone call from someone at Dell Computers based in Austin, Texas. They were asking for a presentation at their head office in Austin. The idea was that their country managers would meet to discuss the annual results and develop their strategy further. It was a late request and there was a big line through my schedule for that particular day, as Ajax were playing in the finals of the European Cup. I usually do my utmost to accommodate clients, but there are limits! I asked my colleague to double my fees to stress to the client that they were dealing with a real pro, one whom you could not just book two weeks in advance. I assumed that the price would be seen as unacceptably high. Within five minutes I got a fax confirming the engagement and the price, as well as a very appreciative word of thanks for my antici-pated contribution. At the time I hardly knew Dell. But all has changed since that occasion. What a great company.

I walked into the breakfast lounge at 6.30 a.m on the day of my presentation, which was to be delivered just after lunchtime. A young man approached me with the words "You have to be Dr Trompenaars; welcome, Fons. Please join me for breakfast." His name tag made it clear that he was a Dell employee and during breakfast we discussed some of the technical details concerning the presentation. The man certainly knew his stuff; perhaps he was the head of technical affairs? Around 7 a.m. many of his colleagues started to trickle in for breakfast and, before sitting at their respective tables, very respectfully greeted my host as "Michael." Could it be that this was Michael Dell himself with whom I had recently discussed the resolution of the beamer? Indeed it was.

During my visit I discovered the tremendous power underlying Dell's business model, fully developed by the founder and main shareholder, Michael Dell. Although he looks like a whizzkid, he has developed into quite a personality over the last ten years, according to his colleagues. What struck me in 1996 was that he had hired a wise and experienced person from Motorola to further develop his successful strategy. Mort Toffler and Michael seemed to have complementary knowledge and experience, and Michael has taken unprecedented advantage of these synergies.

What are the dilemmas that Michael Dell has reconciled? Even before anybody had heard of the Internet, Dell already knew that the intermediate business created too little value and therefore was too costly a model. Add the high quality of his products and logistics and you can understand how he has become one of the richest people in the world in only ten years.

The first dilemma refers to the fact that Dell really understood that the success of organizations in the future is dependant on the ability to develop a business ecosystem. Information products and services are codeveloped for and by participants of the ecosystem. As such, competition and cooperation have organized themselves on a higher level. Such ecosystems cooperate within the system and compete with external ecosystems.

The second dilemma has been reconciled by the genius of Dell's approach, combining direct sales through the Internet to an ever-increasing number of clients in a personal way, with detailed and information-packed services.

A third dilemma that Dell has resolved creatively is the integration of high quality with a reasonable price. Through the perfect application of "mass customization" he has gone beyond the classic dilemma of cheap versus premium strategy. By delivering components at the right time for assembly, he can produce many versions of excellent personal computers without keeping a large stock. Dell has been able to keep the costs low by collating the client's wishes through the Internet in a very cost-effective way.

Dell has reconciled a fourth dilemma by making the personal knowledge previously gained and stored by individual salespeople available to relevant networks of knowledge. The deep and personal insights of local representatives became sources of inspiration for the wider community, with the Internet helping to deepen personal relationships rather than replace them.

Finally, Michael Dell reveals that the most interesting aspect of e-commerce is that people outside the organization, such as suppliers and clients, are taken to the inside and that the inside is thrown to the outside. As he says: "The Internet is used by us as a way to share our applications with both client and supplier in an information partnership." Dell has applied this in Brazil, for example. Customs handling computer parts for assembly in Brazil took much too long for North American standards. Within a year Dell had sold the Brazilian authorities a complete scanning system, for a very good price, that increased the handling speed for the codified products of Intel and other suppliers.

Despite the fact that Dell shares might have decreased significantly over the last couple of years, this approach is not to be measured against quarterly or yearly ups and downs. Dell's business model might well become the focal point of many e-commerce strategies in the next ten years.

TOWARD A BIG BANG

Is there any reader who hasn't looked at one of Bang & Olufsen's audio systems or television sets with great admiration? There are only a few producers of consumer electronics that make such an impressive impact on both the ear as well as the eye. Nevertheless, B&O has faced severe financial problems. Then, in 1991, Anders Knutsen assumed control. He has managed to save a tradition of unequalled industrial design and audio technology from seemingly inescapable ruin. B&O products were so perfect that fewer and fewer people could afford to buy them.

In 1972 the Museum of Modern Art in New York chose to add no fewer than seven B&O products to its permanent collection of modern design. But were audio freaks willing to pay a large amount money for a work of art? And what about art lovers? They did not seem to be willing to acquire so many technological add-ons. More and more it seemed that the combination of design and technology was too high a goal for an organization that was based in Struer, a town of five thousand inhabitants in the north of Denmark, far away from its potential customers. Yet now the organization is not only healthy, but also ready to grow in even more affluent markets.

Turnover has doubled over the last ten years to approximately 500 million euros. Loss has been transformed into a profit of 35 million euros. What did Anders Knutsen do during this period of turn-around? One thing is certain; the concept of integration of design and technology has remained untouched. Closer analysis shows that he has brilliantly reconciled three major dilemmas.

Firstly, Knutsen has reconciled technology push and market pull in a remarkable way. Traditionally, B&O's products are a reflection of the brilliant insights of the technological creativity of Peter Bang and the extrovert sales guru Bengt Olufsen. When the organization was still small the integration of brilliant products and sales to a market that was known in every detail was very natural. After the retirement of the two pioneers many of the functions were professionalized with negative consequences. In that way B&O suited Philips, the Dutch giant, who became the majority shareholder. This led to a guaranteed demand by B&O for Philips components: all very well. The most beautiful designs, made by professional designers such as Jacob Jensen and David Lewis, were stuffed with the most advanced technological delights. There was a small problem, however. They had found the ultimate niche market: that part with no customers.

Anders Knutsen introduced the "butterfly model," with the wings symbolizing respectively R&D, and Marketing and Sales. The dilemma was reconciled by making B&O staff sensitive to sales figures without jeopardizing their creative spirit. Moreover, an increasing number of B&O shops are being established, focusing on selling their own products. Knutsen had found out that B&O products were often used as window dressing, attracting clients to a shop from which they left an hour or so later carrying a Daewoo or Philips. This new approach has led to a dialogue between customers and salespeople that has proven to be extremely profitable.

A second dilemma that Knutsen has taken by the horns is the duality between the ethos of the family in Struer on the one hand – "parents" who were fully trusted – and that of cool rationalism in a global world on the other. The first alternative symbolized a growing family living in abundance; the second stood for a tough, efficient organization which many had to leave. It was crucial that Knutsen, an economist, was able to reconcile both. He managed to secure the support of the whole population of Struer despite the fact that 900 employees had to be dismissed. As the son of the lord of the manor, and based on his honesty and transparency, Knutsen was able to share the pain and to obtain the full support of the village. If an outsider had been hired to implement such a drastic cost reduction program, the whole of the village would have revolted.

A third crucial set of contradicting orientations that Knutsen has been able to integrate is that of technical versus esthetic dominance. B&O has never made concessions to either side and, therefore, manufactured unaffordable products. By the introduction of Idealand, in which engineers, designers, production people, and marketers cooperate, Knutsen has managed to create a synthesis that has saved B&O from financial ruin.

This synthesis of harmonious products that has been achieved in Idealand has been the result of stimulating dialogue between diverse groups of professionals. A couple of times a year an interdisciplinary team goes to the US to get an idea of the latest developments in taste and technology. In this way, a new family of loudspeakers has been developed through the obsession of a musician with the unique noise made by a Harley-Davidson exhaust pipe. Since a sound engineer and a designer participated in this dialog, it was possible to produce a loudspeaker that was much more than an "exhaust pipe," and at a very affordable price.

Knutsen has shown that effective thinking is neither made up of "either/or" nor of "and/and" thinking. Instead dilemmas are reconciled by "through/through" thinking. By better positioning products in the market the company was able to develop better technologies. By being part of the family even tough rational decisions were made acceptable. And finally, through the cooperation of disciplines each was enriched, enabling technological developments through esthetic values.

BOMBARDIER: IN THE CLOUDS WITH A SNOWMOBILE

In just 35 years Laurent Beaudoin has transformed Bombardier, a US$6 million snowmobile company which he took over as a 26 year old from his ailing father-in-law, into an international giant with 50,000 employees in 11 countries and clients in some 60 countries. The company now consists of four divisions, namely recreational products, transport, aerospace, and financial services, with a turnover of more than US$10 billion.

Whilst on my way to a workshop in Montreal involving the top management of Bombardier, I was often congratulated on the fact that I would soon meet the "father of all Canadian managers." And, like all successful leaders, Laurent Beaudoin has approached remarkable dilemmas with great success. How was he able to create an organization now listed number three in aircraft production and sales after Boeing and Airbus, and which is also a world leader in the area of public transportation, from a relatively small company producing ski-doos and sea-doos? It is a remarkable story.

Firstly, Beaudoin, who had originally graduated as an accountant, decided to develop a series of anti-cyclical products on completely intuitive grounds. With the purchase of the Austrian company Lohner-Werke, predominantly for the Rotax as a power source for its recreational products, Bombardier was landed with a public transportation company: a "manufacturer of trams." Rising oil prices in the seventies aided Beaudoin in his decision to apply this unused competence whilst bidding for the renovation of the New York subway. It is common knowledge that public transportation becomes more popular when oil prices increase, and that recreational products take a knock. Beaudoin was able to connect the push of Bombardier's traditional products with a more outward-directed organization, pulled by the market.

A second dilemma that Beaudoin has reconciled is that of the demand for external financiers while maintaining the autonomy of the organization. This is not simple. In situations where everyone has a financial stake it is easy to avoid responsibility. With the financing of large-scale projects such as Eurotunnel and Global Express, Bombardier has always created a community of individuals in which each of the parties has had clear accountability. In this way everyone can take advantage of success and each party is responsible for failure.

The third dilemma is by far the most essential. On the one hand, Bombardier has a family tradition in which hierarchies are well defined and where an "old boy" culture exists. On the other hand, its growth has been dependent on acquisitions where financial rationale and non-traditionalism came first. It would seem that this dilemma is ingrained in the psyche of the former accountant, Laurent Beaudoin. It is to his credit that he was able to acquire companies on the basis of sharp financial calculation and subsequently integrate them with Bombardier on a cultural level. Only a few organizations are able to do that, particularly in the case of unfamiliar industries. Beaudoin has never judged organizations purely on hard financial criteria. He interprets them as value-creating cultures that can help Bombardier unveil the secrets of an industry and the way profits are made in that industry. Because of this relatively few people have lost their jobs after acquisitions. If Beaudoin had simply bought companies on purely short-term business grounds, then he could be called a Global Purchaser. By rejecting the offer to purchase Fokker, he has shown himself as someone who looks further ahead. For me, he is the Purchasing Apprentice who, from the basis of a healthy financial platform, analyses which value-creating capacities other companies can add to his own system. He has proven this with the purchase of LearJet, Havilland, and Short Brothers. These acquisitions went far beyond calculations on the back of an envelope.

A fourth field of tension concerned the need for shared values and processes and entrepreneurship at the divisional level. In his 35 years of leadership Beaudoin always paid attention to the family values of Bombardier, in which entrepreneurship, learning by making mistakes and personal accountability played a crucial part, irrespective of which division people were employed in. Moreover, quality programs such as Six Sigma, used in Bombardier's Engineering, Manufacturing, and IT systems, were centrally designed and carried out. An additional source of energy for internal consistency is a number of cross-divisional forums, in which "best practices" are continuously exchanged. All these systems are effective because of the autonomy of Bombardier's divisions.

Finally, Beaudoin's workmanship has transformed a family company into an unequalled meritocracy. He would never have become a leader if he had not married the daughter of the founder of Bombardier. In previous works I have contrasted ascribed status with status gained on the basis of what people have achieved for themselves. At Bombardier, Beaudoin himself – with his ascribed status – has time and time again shown his colleagues the importance of achievement. In this way, as in companies such as Motorola and Mars, ascribed status becomes a platform from which one can achieve. This is confirmed by the fact that in healthy companies, like Bombardier, family members need to achieve more than people brought in from the outside. That will not be easy for Beaudoin's son who at the moment is managing the least profitable division – Recreation.

It is also striking that while I was returning to the airport and sharing my enthusiasm with the driver about Laurent Beaudoin's achievements, he whispered that he didn't know that Monsieur Beaudoin had a son. In Canada one speaks of *Monsieur* Beaudoin, never Laurent.

PARADOXES AT APPLIED MATERIALS

The American company Applied Materials was recently awarded a prestigious prize for the best product (Quantum Leap System) in the semi-conductor industry, presented by *Semiconductor International Magazine*. However, it isn't just the quality of the company's products that is worth noting. Even in 1997, when I was invited to speak at its quarterly top management meeting, it was obvious that I was not dealing with an ordinary organization. Many American companies that claim to be "international" are often international only on the outside, but are wholly American deep within. Management team photographs portraying foreigners surrounding the "white core" of the organization often illustrate this fact. AMAT, on the contrary, is the most international company I have met so far, and I have been privileged to work with them.

The top 50 people at AMAT represent 30 different nationalities. There is a German marketing director, a Japanese human resources vice-president, and many heads of country are locals. Another crucial figure in this culturally diverse management whole is Dan Maydan, an Israeli scientist who started it all with Jim Morgan, an American businessman who today is AMAT's CEO.

AMAT is the world's largest manufacturer of semiconductor instruments, machines that produce microchips. For those of you who are still not convinced of the important role this organization and its leaders play in our economy today, listen closely to what market observers have said about AMAT. They have gone as far as to state that the world economy would suffer a greater loss if AMAT stopped its production for a few months than if Intel closed down completely. Since the company's foundation its turnover has increased from US$100,000 to US$5 billion, with profits amounting to US$750 million.

How did Jim Morgan manage to achieve all this? How did he manage to create wealth from cultural diversity? In an interview which my colleague Peter Prud'homme and I had with him, he talked of

the ways in which his employees have effectively dealt with paradoxes and dilemmas. Using this capability AMAT first penetrated
the Japanese market: Morgan believes that, if an organization is able
to conquer the most difficult country in the world, namely Japan,
then it will be able to access Europe and the rest of Asia more easily.
Jim described this valuable insight in his book *Cracking the Japanese
Market.*

He says that "Globalization ideally starts with cultures that differ as
much as possible with your local markets." It is only then that one
can successfully manage dilemmas, and he identifies some seven
dilemmas that AMAT has cleverly reconciled.

Errors and corrections. It is striking to see how much value Jim Morgan attaches to making errors as a way of learning. AMAT has introduced several error-correcting systems as one of the means of
continuous business improvement.

Extensive participation with satisfied customers and making fast decisions.
Jim Morgan knows that the true secret of leadership lies in combining participation in decision making with efficient consultation.

Excellent technology and effective production systems. Because AMAT
takes full responsibility for total system integration and does not just
produce a machine, it also caters for the man-machine interface and
the final result of the entire system.

Local fit and global reach. Jim Morgan does not believe in slogans such
as "act local and think global," because they are essentially empty.
Within AMAT he has highlighted the underlying issue in this particular dilemma, namely cross-cultural competence. As a result of

this he ensures that virtually everything at AMAT is done in transnational teams. According to him, these cross-cultural teams are a reflection of the diversity of the organization itself – and its clients.

Stable continuity and flexible change. This dilemma is the nightmare of every leader. The values that the organization stands for are clearly demonstrated through its leaders, but within these boundaries each person can have complete freedom. Jim Morgan believes that everybody at AMAT should demonstrate world-class performance in everything that they do, and believes that this is only possible if one is close to the client. He also believes that it is important to show trust and respect in everything you do.

Growing bigger and remaining small. The synthesis between big and small is accomplished by integrating modular thinking and action. Each module represents a "Total Solution" that can be applied in a very flexible manner by combining modules in a unique way.

Viewing from on high and going in deep – AMAT's "porpoise style" leadership. One of Jim Morgan's characteristic competencies is his ability to join a long-term strategic view with short-term tactical capacities. Because his long-term thinking is integrated in the full picture, all his short-term initiatives form part of a meaningful context. By shifting between the long- and short-term perspectives, he knows how to avoid daydreaming and focusing on irrelevancies.

Although Jim Morgan and AMAT may not be very well known names, this organization and its leader are exemplary. The manner in which Jim Morgan has reconciled his dilemmas could well be symbolic for the leadership of this century.

RICHARD BRANSON'S VIRGIN LEADERSHIP

The essential competence of leaders is the ability to integrate opposing values; that is my central statement. A master in this area is Richard Branson of Virgin. Which dilemmas has he reconciled to become so successful?

The context in which Branson has integrated seemingly opposing values contains three elements. First of all, he has managed to unify the Virgin brand with his own personality. Secondly, he has turned his businesses into a moral activity: The values of Virgin are based on personal gain, but are at the service of the common good. These are demonstrated by such things as the introduction of cheap condoms at the beginning of the AIDS epidemic and the launch of airships for the aerial detection of landmines. Finally, Branson has used the typical British characteristics of irony and humor, not sparing himself. Take, for example, a story from his autobiography, *Losing My Virginity*. He and his family were catching their breath in Mallorca immediately after winning the lawsuit against British Airways. He had been all over the media for weeks. At the edge of the swimming pool, surrounded by newspapers full of positive comments and photographs of him, a couple asked him to take a picture. After he had obligingly tidied his hair it turned out to be a misunderstanding. "No, sir," they explained, "would you be so kind as to take a picture of *us*?"

This combination of personality, moral responsibility, and irony make him a tough cookie for his opponents to crack; he remains a moving target. They are also the means that enable Branson to be very effective in dealing with the following dilemmas.

Making money and turning the economic system around. Whether it is the superior service of Virgin Atlantic threatening the monopoly of British Airways from Gatwick and Heathrow, or the introduction of Virgin Cola in competition to Coca-Cola and Pepsi, the principle is the same. It also applies to the introduction of Virgin Direct, an alternative way of Internet banking without the expensive services of middlemen, and to launching a service that allows the British to import cars from the continent. All Branson's services have the following common denominator: Established companies are forced not only to adjust their prices but also, in most cases, to transform their business model by offering a creative alternative. This is always closely observed by the media, who generally cheer on Branson, the underdog.

Profit for shareholders and stakeholders. A second dilemma that Branson has reconciled is a classic one. He has managed to integrate the interest of the shareholders and other stakeholders by making his employees, who take great satisfaction from serving their customers, fellow shareholders. By doing this he has created a model in which there is a balance between all concerned.

Specific purposes in a diffuse context. Dyslexia, from which Branson suffers, has led to him delegating some specific aspects and the numbers of the business to people he trusts. He has managed to neutralize his own shortcoming by developing a strong social intelligence. Virgin Atlantic does not only ask whether you would like a neck massage while on board, but also ensures that there is a limousine waiting for you at JFK. A chauffeur of one of those limousines told me the other day that his tips were extremely high, because of the degree of satisfaction of the customers. Branson allies himself with partners who know the specific details of a business and he makes them part of a bigger, more diffuse whole. This is illustrated by fact that Branson is known as a very tough negotiator, a haggler who could put a Turkish carpet dealer to shame. However, when there is the possibility of making some money, Branson will spend it to further the interests of the customer – not his own.

Mature businesses and enduring entrepreneurial spirit. How does Branson continuously manage to unite a mature and very profitable organization with enduring entrepreneurship? Part of the answer lies in the structure of the organization that he has developed. It consists of many independent small businesses, which are part of a network controlled by twenty people in head office. Many of these small companies are start-ups originating in bright ideas which have been dreamed up by Virgin's own people. He assesses some fifty proposals a week and will give each of them three months to get off the ground. If things go well, he gives them his full support; if they don't work out, he pulls the plug. For example, the idea of Bridal Services – covering everything related to weddings – originated in the fertile imagination of a Virgin Atlantic stewardess. After a short conversation with Branson she was able to start.

The winning antagonist and the pitiful underdog. The final dilemma that Branson has managed to reconcile is very interesting. From his childhood onwards Branson has learnt to be – and not to play at – David fighting Goliath. Many giants still regret this. Because he takes up good causes whenever he can he manages to take advantage of each dispute. If he wins, as against British Airways, this is clear. However, if he loses, as with his bid for the National Lottery in the UK, he still knows how to turn it into a victory by either manipulating public opinion or by being in the public eye. My favorite leader is Richard Branson. Why? Because he has introduced a new kind of capitalism, one in which human beings are central.

WHEN TURKISH DELIGHT BECOMES VALUABLE FOR EUROPE

The process of European integration is already taxing for Western countries. What will this process mean for the countries to the east, ranging from Poland to Turkey? European access and globalization are high on the agendas of the political leaders of these countries. Can the business world play a role in this difficult task?

When my colleague Jo Spyckerelle interviewed Rahmi M. Koç, the current owner and president of the Turkish Koç Group of companies, it became clear how far away Turkish culture is from the need for transparency felt by the New Europe and the international business environment.

The Turkey-based Koç Group is an interesting case, because for the last 75 years it has been very successful in its own territory. Is that sufficient, however, to also be able to compete on a global scale? Rahmi Koç took over the reins of the family business from his father at the age of 65. Vehbi Koç, founder of the Koç dynasty, stayed on as honorary chairman until he died in 1996 at the age of 94. During his 70-year reign, Vehbi established a conglomerate that in itself represents almost 6 percent of the Turkish GNP. Over 45,000 staff are involved in activities ranging from mining, car assembly, and heavy industry to tourism and financial services.

Against the backdrop of a striking view of the Bosphorus, Rahmi

Koç talked about the dilemmas facing him: Tensions throwing an entirely different light on the process of internationalization.

A first dilemma relates to maintaining close and loyal family ties in the succession process versus the demands put by the Western financial establishment on Koç's public shares. "The strength of our organization is the loyalty of its people," stated Rahmi Koç, whose three sisters each manage a substantial part of the business. In order to fulfil international demands, Koç will need to go public and to become fully transparent. The tensions this created were clearly revealed when Koç pulled out of its attempt to be quoted on the New York Stock Exchange in 1998. According to Rahmi Koç, it was particularly difficult to translate a local reputation into global financial criteria. Add to this the weak reputation of Eastern companies (especially after the Asian crisis), and conglomerates in particular, and the valuation gap between the US$2.2 billion estimated by the American investors and the US$5.6 billion of their own evaluation is easily understood. "A lot of the values of a family business, the long-term loyalty to our country, our environment, our consumers, our suppliers, and the value of a lifelong reputation for integrity went unnoticed by global investors. We felt substantially depreciated before the eyes of the world," said Rahmi Koç.

How can one reconcile this dilemma? Western criteria for transparency do turn a blind eye towards immeasurable qualities such as loyalty, reputation and "know-who," which make up the essential strength of a Turkish organization. Rahmi Koç will have to turn the family's reputation into the main enticement for the Wall Street investor. Koç's success stories, evinced by more than twenty alliances with companies such as Fiat, Ford, fashion businesses like Mexx, and retail organizations such as Migros, will need to serve as examples for the value represented by diffuse orientations and links with the government and other parties in Turkey.

Which brings us to a second, similar theme. Will Koç, despite its regionally impressive size, market share, and financial means, be able to withstand the competitive pressure of global players? Koç has become big in Turkey, and the Turkish economy has for the past twenty years been rather closed. As long as Koç controls many local loyalties, it will be quite hard for international companies to penetrate the Turkish market. Western and Eastern businesses will need to establish alliances on the basis of equality with regards to strategy, production techniques, and market intelligence. In this way, they can effectively initiate a learning process between all the alliance partners.

Equally, Koç plays an important role in balancing public and private interest. The Turkish government is still the largest employer in the country. As in many other cases, this does not always mean the most effective use of resources. Koç has, next to creating many non-profit foundations, also been involved in the management of these organizations. If a local, Koç-sponsored school is not being managed by one of its directors, care is taken to locate it close to one of the Koç plants, so the company can keep a close watch on the school's quality.

What should Rahmi Koç do with the dilemma that the most successful economies have their origins in a free-market system, while Turkey is still a state economy? Although some dilemmas are difficult to resolve when one lacks power, Rahmi Koç still discerns possibilities of using his influence. The Koç Group has a large number of highly educated staff, who are not only committed to Koç but also to the Turkish state, and in the long run, the initiative will need to come from them. The flip side of this coin is that patriotism in Turkey can degenerate into a narrow form of nationalism.

To a great extent Turkey's future is in the hands of leaders such as Rahmi Koç. His country and his organization belong neither to the universe of the Jihad, nor to that of McWorld. There is an opportunity for us in the West to enjoy this kind of Turkish Delight: a dessert made up of loyalty and long-term vision, one that requires a great deal of farsightedness and courage.

HOW REFRESHING, HOW VUURSTEEN

It is not easy to manage a company which has such a long family tradition as Heineken. Its success is indeed connected with the way values and meanings are constantly being fine-tuned as circumstances change.

My colleague Dirk Devos interviewed Karel Vuursteen on the dilemmas he has managed to overcome as CEO of Heineken, but these were not only about the reconciliation of company and family interests. This first, and probably most crucial, dilemma has been in the news repeatedly, because of the discussion about whether Freddy Heineken's holding should or should not be dissolved. Vuursteen has managed to balance the tension between the long-term interests of the family and the usually more short-term interests of investors. This is a tension which would improve the health of many organizations.

Vuursteen has often been characterized as a person who proposes too careful a policy. Nevertheless, it is a policy that has established an effective balance between risky, thoughtless growth and careful, slow shrinkage. Managing this tension has resulted in an average nominal growth of 14 percent per annum since 1980. Many organizations would be jealous of that.

He has also earned his spurs in a second field of tension. Although many advised him to exploit the Heineken brand to the utmost, others whispered that the strength actually lay within the brewer technology. However, Vuursteen did not consider this a choice. This successful brewer has one of the few premium beers in the world with a global presence. On the other hand, beer is a regional product par excellence as far as taste and production processes are concerned, and Heineken appears to succeed in promoting a more regional, mouth-to-mouth appeal.

If you take a closer look at Heineken's strategy, you will see that it tackles this dilemma in a clever way. It takes over local breweries and has a lot of experience in transferring its knowledge in the areas of brewer technologies and distribution, while local taste and tradition are respected. Local sales points, customers, and goodwill are being used optimally in this process. When all these conditions are fulfilled, Heineken connects its global brand and image to the entity that has been acquired. This approach offers Heineken the opportunity of integrating low costs and premium products, so that the customer may be offered a wider choice.

Whereas the Belgian company Interbrew and South African Breweries (SAB) mostly invest in brewer techniques and distribution and Anheuser Busch throws itself into a brand policy with Budweiser and Corona, Heineken integrates both. This "decentralized coordination" allowed Vuursteen to integrate the local roots of the beers with a global first class brand.

Finally, Vuursteen must have lost some sleep over the battle between tradition and stability on the one hand, and the call for innovation and new products on the other. For many years now Heineken's success has been unequalled. It is obvious that customers love Heineken, but the reason why is actually less clear. Launching new products without really knowing why the people who drink Heineken are so loyal would carry too many risks.

To reconcile this dilemma Vuursteen has chosen two relatively safe types of innovation. First, constant attention is given to process innovations searching for more effective tools which may lead to the same results. Secondly, active encouragement is given, leaving room for creativity, to provide the opportunity of creating new drinks from scratch without jeopardizing Heineken's tradition of premium products. It's a little bit like Volkswagen, which started building the Golf while the Beetle was still popular.

SIMPLICITY WITH A SMILE

Kees Storm, President of the Board of AEGON, together with Vink of CSM, is a leader who combines simplicity with Dutch acuteness and shrewdness. Storm has developed his own tricks. He is known to insiders for his unusual way of inspiring people through laying bets. He wagers with colleagues on the objectives set for a relevant unit. Storm will give a good bottle of wine whenever targets are made or exceeded. When Storm loses, AEGON has won. This is typical of Kees Storm. He wants to traumatize losing and ensure that people enjoy beating him. Winning something from your boss is great.

Since 1998 the market value of AEGON has doubled. Looking back to 1990 we see that Storm's management has contributed in part to the present value of the shares – which are now thirty times higher than in that year. So what dilemmas has Storm turned into win–win situations? Two are particularly remarkable. Their resolution has led to the integration of many other opposing values.

AEGON's organization has been radically decentralized so that it can react to the judicial and cultural peculiarities of local markets. Local units have been encouraged to exceed Storm's bets, which will then be discussed by a small group of specialists (finance, IT, and other functional experts) to analyze which results are comparable and which ones are unique. While differences are respected, Storm has also continuously motivated the organization to look for consistency among the units.

It is remarkable how quickly AEGON has managed to exchange and duplicate best practices. In this case the need for consistency and comparison (how else can people place these bets?) has been reconciled on a higher level with the effectiveness of local adjustments and autonomy.

Storm has ensured that the role of the head office remains limited to facilitating this integration. For one thing, three times a year the complete Management Board visits the operational units to present AEGON's strategy and to listen to what is happening at the local level. In this way all 30,000 employees, independent of their rank or station, have the opportunity to comment or question the Board.

Nobody in AEGON can say that they have not had a chance, on a regular basis, of addressing Kees Storm or another member of the Board personally. Nor is Storm the type of person to create any obstacles to accepting this invitation. This policy is feasible because Storm has chosen not to expand into more than the ten countries in which AEGON wants to be a dominant player.

The small focus groups of specialists, the regular meetings and the wagers for the best results are just a few example of the many ways in which AEGON has managed to encourage the different units to inspire each other and learn. It is, however, a complex process in which some diversities are singled out and others are avoided, like mixing bank and insurance activities.

Furthermore Storm – together with Vink of CSM – features among my favorite leaders, because both emphatically do not hold with shareholder value. Storm is even irritated by the stupidity of this monolithic concept. He believes that creating value starts with the customer. That is AEGON's primary task, which can only be realized by motivated employees performing to the best of their ability because they are provided with the appropriate means. According to Storm the latter is only possible if employees have access to the right resources.

Creating value concerns many stakeholders and one of the expressions of leadership is finding the right balance between all their interests. Whenever one interest is predominant it becomes a vicious circle. Storm has shown that it is possible to create a learning spiral in which all the varied interests contribute in spinning the wheel to greater heights. This is only possible when the interests of shareholders, employees, society, and clients follow naturally on from each other. To facilitate this process AEGON has launched a share option scheme, integrating all interests. Everyone within the organization is encouraged to participate in this program; 90 percent have already done so.

I still remember a workshop at AEGON University. We had a discussion about the dress code for the final dinner, which Kees Storm would attend. All the Dutch members opted for orange outfits; they were definitely going to beat the Italians that night in the semi-finals of the Euro 2000 football tournament. Out of respect for the chairman the majority of the people from other countries were in favor of a more formal dress code.

The Dutch representative couldn't resist contacting Kees Storm and asking him for his opinion. His reply was simple: "Dress as you like, then I will do so too." He arrived wearing an orange tie, coordinating perfectly with his suit. The Dutch as well as the foreigners had another story to tell and everyone felt respected, even the Dutch, since a tie in the color of the losing team was more than they could expect.

CLUB MED: BUILDING A VACATION DREAM

The guiding spirit of Club Méditerranée, Gilbert Trigano, died recently. In 1950, after the Belgian Gérard Blitz founded the company, Trigano distributed tents to the first non-profit holiday organization at Mallorca. Trigano, the youngest son of a rich Jewish-Algerian family, delivered the tents for a small part of the turnover of the organization started by Blitz. A few years later, in 1953, Blitz and Trigano combined their forces and Club Med was a fact.

The idea was to join Gentils Organisateurs (GOs) together with Gentils Membres (GMs or holidaymakers) in activities ranging from sports to washing the dishes. Since then quite a bit has changed in the concept of this all-in package holiday organization. Club Med now has 129 villages, 8,000 GOs, and 30,000 employees who together generate a turnover of US$2 billion. During the nineties Club Med went through several bad years. Trigano's son Serge was unable to turn this around in 1993. The Agnelli family, the majority shareholders, therefore appointed Philippe Bourguignon to rescue the Club. His task was to make the largest sports and holiday resort profitable again without losing the vision of Gilbert Trigano. This vision was to make people happy in an egalitarian environment where "vous" always became the less formal "tu."

After his successful turnaround at Euro Disney, Philippe Bourguignon found a dilapidated Club Med. In most villages repairs were considerably overdue and it seemed that costs were of no importance, ensuring that customers were kept in unnecessary luxury. A weekly firework spend of about US$12,000 was not exceptional. The biggest challenge for Bourguignon was to keep the good things of French life without the unnecessary, but also French, luxury and grandeur.

The unequalled success of Club Med can be credited to several distinguishing characteristics of French culture, as well as its capacity to integrate values in such a way that the competition had thought impossible. As the founder Blitz himself said: "It's a strange cocktail of living in a castle and in nature simultaneously." Trigano added to this typical French contradictions such as pride and being "au naturel," individualism and camaraderie, a mixture of sport, sensuality, culture and exotic décors, a yearly flight away from the stresses of society, and a utopian brotherhood.

It seemed that the dilemmas Bourguignon had to solve were a mirror image of his successful job at Euro Disney, where he had to introduce a typical American concept that had to be accepted by the French. Club Med had to reconcile expensive French contradictions with American efficiency. Which dilemmas did Bourguignon solve to become profitable again?

The first one was a strategic dilemma of the first order. On the one hand Club Med had created the expectation on the part of the customer of unequalled personal service. Since this became unaffordable, the specter was raised of a product that was affordable and reliable, but which was also standardized and global. During the last three years Bourguignon has managed to rationalize several ingredients based on Club Med's core values, such as 10 instead of 20 different choices on the menu, the fireworks and the weekly champagne festival upon arrival and departure, and has integrated them into an arrangement aimed at achieving tasteful "esprit et ambiance." The unnecessary costs of certain elements have been cut while managing to maintain or even increase the luxury. Of course, Bourguignon understood that real taste is inexpensive. It was the values of the nouveau riche that had harmed profits.

Bourguignon found a very strong brand that had lately become ambivalent. Customers expected dreams that could not possibly be made to come true. He solved this dilemma by once again marketing all products under a single brand. He has cleverly chosen the regeneration of body and mind as the main theme, and in the process Club Med has been resurrected. According to Bourguignon the tourist industry is no longer a side dish. We no longer entertain ourselves from the sidelines; entertainment has now become an essential part of mankind's experience. The branding of Club Med has turned the holiday game into a serious business that combines hard ingredients with a worldly imagination.

The third dilemma is about rationalization while at the same time conserving something that is unique. During his rescue operation at Euro Disney Philippe Bourguignon was considered too American by the French, who happen to love the unique and the unpredictable. Rationalization would cause Club Med to loose its aura of adventure. The appraisal of the "chefs de village" was not based on this scale. Developing new shows (with an Oscar as a trophy) and satisfied customers were the priorities in the past, leading to financial disaster. Bourguignon introduced a balanced scorecard, by which the performance of rejuvenated local management was reviewed. Client satisfaction was balanced with management's performance on targets, budget, and profits. This change motivated management to create satisfied customers by generating profits. Since a smarter off-season pricing policy, increased mobility of personnel between the various resorts, and a more professional booking system complemented this change, it is clear that the sympathetic Bourguignon has managed another success story. Club Med is finally without losses.

THE FAMILY IN BUSINESS OR BUSINESS IN THE FAMILY?

Most businesses are small to medium-sized enterprises, providing most of the employment and innovation in the world. Small enterprises are also the little seeds out of which huge trees can grow. In addition it seems that many of the governments in the G8 are trying to preserve the creative spirit of small to medium-sized enterprises with tax advantages and other supporting regulations.

Let us assume that family businesses and small to medium-sized enterprises are the same: businesses employing less than 200 people and having a turnover of less than US$20 million. In most cases management, property, and shareholders are closely related. In 1996 an article in *The Economist* stated that small to medium-sized enterprises accounted for 40 percent of the American and 66 percent of the German GNP. Besides this, it turns out that these small businesses are important for employment: employing 60 percent in America, 75 percent in Germany and England, 80 percent in Spain and 85–90 percent in Switzerland.

Why is it that the family business is so prosperous and successful? A study by Leach (1994) shows that each dollar invested in a family business in 1970 had a value of a little more than $11 in 1990, while investing in public funding would have given a return of about $9. This success can be attributed to the reconciliation of a number of cultural dilemmas. However, not everyone is buying this: 18 percent of American and 25 percent of European family businesses don't reach the third generation.

The most important dilemma is described in a study by Swaffin-Smith, Woolliams and Tomenko (2000) as being that between family and business interests. The main motive of family interests (the "Livelihood Business") is to skim off personal gain from the professional success of the organization. Most of the time this is used for educating family members or financing the home, and family members are better paid than outsiders, with children often feeling pressurized into joining the family business. In this model, this even happens in situations where there are better skilled people on the open labor market: Family first, even at the cost of the business. There are only a few family businesses like this that survive past the second generation.

We also have the model in which business motives are predominant, called the "Independent Business." Management has its own autonomy and will often ask family members to support the company, even if this is damaging to the reputation or interests of one of the family. Business and family are kept strictly apart. Financing in this model often takes place from several sources with a clear understanding of mid- and long-term yield and is guided by an external accountant. There will be a clear business strategy with a focus on expansion; the family is viewed as a possible source of finance or human talent, but there is no automatic mechanism. This usually means heavy pressure on family relations and reputations, followed by divorce or similar family tragedies. That is why we often observe a definite split between the family and the business after the second generation.

A typical compromise between business and family interests may be called "Lifestyle Business." In this case a balance is sought between both ends, making this, also, not the most ideal model.

A fourth type, the "Immortality Business" model, combines business as well as family interests on a higher level, leading to the most successful family businesses. It is the only model in which organizations survive past the third generation. However, it needs leaders who are able to reconcile some major dilemmas. First of all, leaders of family businesses have greater flexibility than their equals in larger bureaucracies. It seems that their success is determined by the fact that extended room for maneuver is circumscribed by a clearly stated set of values. The family Fentener van Vlissingen at SHV and Makro is a good example. This is an organization in which values have permeated the organization for many generations. These values often rise above the individual level and challenge family members to live up to their responsibilities.

This last model distinguishes itself from less successful family businesses, because it uses the tension between the founders and their prestige-oriented successors. The founders areimmortal because they have created a culture in which family members have been faced with higher demands in order to qualify as successors. The American family company Mars is a good example of this as well. Sons and daughters of multiple brothers and sisters are assessed on their competencies and only the best make it to the top. Short-term gain is of less importance than long-term goals. The history of the family is fully integrated into the history of the company, and everybody approves.

It is a pity that fewer and fewer family businesses survive. The desire to make money fast above long-term stakeholder value has also gained the upper hand in family business.

CHAPTER 3

Matching values

Why do the majority of mergers and acquisitions fail? How is it that, though the importance of the cultural factor is widely recognized, so little is done in terms of any cultural due diligence? And what are the dilemmas created in a cross-border alliance?

FEELINGS ARE FACTS

A recent report by the Boston Consulting Group confirms that a large number (30 percent) of mergers and acquisitions are of less value than anticipated. Culture turns out to be one of the most relevant factors. Is that surprising? No, not really; most people would have thought it. What, however, is truly striking is the big difference between this report and similar research done by KPMG, where 70 percent were found to be unsuccessful. It is also interesting to note that, based on the analysis of a number of recent European mergers and acquisitions, cultural differences are not only national but also industry-specific.

The difference in percentages is probably related to the criteria used to judge whether an integration is successful or not. An initial analysis of the two reports quickly reveals a difference in approach. Boston Consulting's report uses shareholder-only language: Wealth creation is measured by evaluating the benefits to shareholders (as I have said before, they are those who never share). The KPMG approach is more from the stakeholder point of view, concerning the interest of more parties and including subjective feelings and the perceptions of others rather than only those of the financially interested parties. Where Boston Consulting considers a marriage only successful if children are produced, KPMG appear to have more sympathy with the idea that love would be great, too! On this note, it may be interesting to refer to an analysis of the failure of Chrysler in the *Wall Street Journal*, appearing in November 2000, which only looked at the economic point of view. There was no word on the role of Schremmp or on differing German and American cultures, but only on the wrong investment in research and development and on launching the wrong models at the wrong time. Fortunately another article on the subject which appeared in the *Japan Times* at the same time balanced this by stating clearly that the problems were mainly at a cultural level – the headline was "Plan to oust Daimler-Chrysler chief exposes trans-Atlantic cultural rift."

I remember the interesting discussions around the possible merger of Samsung and Fokker. It seemed that the Dutch had not progressed further than legal and financial analyses, whereas Samsung, even in the first instance, wanted to get to the heart of Dutch culture. Yes, these are simply different points of view, but different points of view that can lead to serious misunderstandings. It would be much more interesting to look at which specific interactions between partners were damaging or, conversely, constructive. One could do a lot with the diverging perceptions people have of each other, for in perceptions we find meaning – the perception of the potential partner and the perception of your own organization, and that those cultures are systems of shared perception. It is by discussing different perceptions that values are created in marriages and also in mergers and acquisitions, and therein lies the most significant opportunity of distinguishing yourself from other mergers and acquisitions. Clarify mutual perceptions clearly and reconcile them at a higher level.

Finally, let's make a note in the margin to the effect that industry-specific differences should be more important than national differences. Our experience at Trompenaars Hampden-Turner, supported by our database of 65,000 respondents, teaches that organizational culture is indeed an important variable that can dictate whether a merger or acquisition will succeed or fail. But national culture can explain a lot of misery as well. In my experience it is much more interesting to look at the relationship between different cultural factors, allowing national culture within organizational culture to play a more significant role. When Volvo negotiated with Renault, the national role of Volvo in Sweden turned out to be much more important than any differences in corporate culture. If we correctly interpret the signals from Daimler and Chrysler, organizational and national cultures strengthen each other, and the personality of the leader plays an important role. In the case of Vodafone and Mannesman, national cultures appeared to strengthen the organizational culture.

However, some people would say that even an unfriendly takeover can create value. Correct. But we also know how many highly talented staff can walk out and how many frustrations and personal dramas can take place. Value is created on many levels; that is why it is so critical for perceptions to be taken into account.

WHEN TWO WORLDS COLLIDE

Many things go wrong in alliance country. At DaimlerChrysler many talented American managers have chosen to leave. If we look at how much value was destroyed at Reed Elsevier, then it is time that one starts thinking in a fundamentally different way about alliances.

Globalization through mergers, acquisitions and strategic alliances is big business – currently well over US$2,000 billion annually, according to *The Economist*. Relational aspects like cultural differences and lack of trust turn out to be responsible for a large percentage of alliance failures. Problems can be due to more or less "objective" cultural differences, but also to perceptions about each other, including perceptions of corporate culture and national culture. In short, culture is pervasive. These complex processes are important not only for the implementation of internationalization strategies, but also because of the consequences of political, monetary, and legal convergence. Nevertheless, two out of three marriages produce considerably less than what one hoped for at the wedding ceremony.

My experience has taught me that a lot of acquisition failures can be blamed on insufficient attention being paid to the human factor. Of course an integration program must be based on technical and financial factors, but these need to be applied within a cultural framework. As we have seen in the KPMG study of alliances, 70 percent of failing mergers and acquisitions can be attributed to relational factors such as cultural misunderstandings between the parties involved. Sometimes these have little to do with national cultural differences. Problems with the alliance between Sony and Philips, for example, were particularly caused by the market focus of Sony, which made the technocrats of Philips extremely nervous.

Most managers have been aware of these facts for quite some time, but they also know, on intuitive grounds, that during the integration process they need to take into account several management styles, organizational structures, work classifications, and decision-making processes. Knowing all this, how is it possible that so much attention is given to financial and technical aspects, whereas "cultural due diligence" is still hardly used? Cultural surveys are vital, and they need to be based on the three steps of recognition, respect, and reconciliation.

At the first step of recognition, awareness, one needs to work cautiously. Do not stop at the external artefacts of culture such as the organization chart, the personnel handbook, or the dress code on Friday. I saw the problems this could cause a few years ago, when KLM and Alitalia were in negotiation. Lots of attention was given to the long socks of the Italians and the buttermilk of the Dutch. If workshops are given on this basic level, then one runs the risk that preconceived stereotypes are confirmed: "You see, those Dutch have no taste," and "I knew it, Italians only focus on their appearance."

The two parties need to touch on much deeper assumptions, and here one needs to focus on behavior resulting from frequently solved dilemmas. These solutions have become routines that, like breathing, have become automatic. These deeper assumptions need to be addressed through a cultural due diligence during the first steps in alliances.

Within alliances it is then important to develop a respect for the differences encountered. This second step is too important to ignore, as too frequently happens with futile workshops where participants from different cultures are taught about the differences between them in separate rooms. As before, these generally lead to strengthening already existing stereotypes. Respect starts with understanding the origin of differences, and frequently concludes with the observation that the others are simply "people like us." Once parties have charted the differences and come to respect them, life changes into one big dilemma.

Hence the third step, reconciliation, which concerns the incorporation of the most important opposing orientations. Slowly the conviction grows that one adds value in an alliance by the integration of seemingly opposing values. However, this is not often a success, especially if one partner sticks to their values and proclaims "mine first." Jurgen Schremmp at DaimlerChrysler seems to be a supporter of that approach. But a compromise between both partners can also lead to disappointing results. We have also observed many alliances where both parties preserve their own values and build a "living apart together" relationship where they exist at arm's length. But we have found that effective alliances are possible, and they are those where values are continuously integrated. In this process partners jointly work on the creation of a new culture transcending their own values.

As Edgar Schein has stated in *Organizational Cultures and Leadership*, this integration process is fully dependent on the quality and the will of leadership. In *The Leadership Challenge* the Americans Kouzes and Posner have clearly shown how essential it is to align linking activities with the comprehensive strategy of the new organization. It is of the utmost importance to develop a code or conduct as well as common business principles. Subsequently, the two parties need to define the most important cultural dilemmas that affect the effectiveness of the organization. Thus the new alliance can reconcile seemingly opposing values.

The process of "reconciliation" (here we refer to the dictionary meaning of the active process of integrating seemingly opposing values) has been developed by Charles Hampden-Turner. His approach assumes that several parties interact, so that a new reality is created in which values are defined on a higher level. This is something quite different from the creation of a context where one talks about the importance of wearing long socks or drinking buttermilk!

One of the most often recurring dilemmas concerns the difference in customer relationships. These are obvious between Italians and Dutch, but also between British and Americans. It is typically American to choose a very specific service. On American flights shorter than two hours no breakfast is served. More than once, as a first class-passenger, I have protested at the terrible choice between potato chips and small pretzels at seven o'clock in the morning. The contrast is huge if you then fly with British Airways or Singapore Airlines. During short flights from Amsterdam to London I get offered a hot breakfast with champagne. In the alliance between American Airlines and British Airways there is one option for integrating these seemingly opposing orientations into a new corporate culture – the compromise of serving a hot pretzel. But differences can be reconciled more sensibly.

If you give full service to everyone, unconditionally, you go bankrupt as many Japanese banks have done. If you give unlimited service all the way up until the moment when the customer really needs it, then you will lose out against the competition. The process of reconciliation is about defining the specific areas where you as an airline company, say, can give more personal service. Jan Carlzon of SAS called this integration "moments of truth," indicating the importance of a conscious choice.

The added, or rather integrated value, of an alliance will depend on the effectiveness of the process of reconciliation. The parties involved must look where they are going creatively; a compromise is killing. When partners engage in a reconciliation process, a joint and new reality will be created.

YOU'RE AN IDIOT, BUT DON'T TAKE IT PERSONALLY

After their unlucky courtship with Alitalia, mentioned above, KLM looked to British Airways. In the area of culture many such Anglo-Dutch combinations provide a wealth of experience, and there have been lots of opportunities for cultural analyses, many more than in the case of Italy.

Had the acquisition by BA actually happened, there would have been a good chance of the integration succeeding on a cultural basis. As we have seen in the cases of Shell and Unilever the British and the Dutch are able to create synergies. Yes, success is closely dependent on factors such as leadership, corporate culture, objectives, and size, but if it the area of culture does not function, then the chances of success are very limited.

What is so interesting about Anglo-Dutch partnerships? It isn't just that the British make jokes and the Dutch laugh. Nor is it the long British preparatory sessions for projects, which are then executed by the Dutch, or the British "process thinking" and the Dutch "content focus." What works is the subtle balance between similar cultural values and their complementarity, where there are any differences.

Firstly it should be clear that, in the case of British Airways we are talking about an British company, not the British people as a whole.

The Dutch and the English appear to score similarly on a number of cultural characteristics. Both are universalistic, which can also cause problems as this Protestant orientation often leads to an "one best way of doing things" attitude, which begs the question of whose "best" will be used. The English and the Dutch share common experiences in the fields of trade, bartering, and creative financial management, all deriving from the notion of money as a universal commodity that needs an open market in order to thrive. The same, of course, is true of the Scottish and the Dutch – and Shell and Unilever show how successful these combinations can be.

In addition, both the Dutch and the English understand the concept of the gentleman's agreement, that is, that once somebody has agreed to do something, there is no need to write it down. In negotiations this can cause big problems. The question is not whether both parties want one standard; both of them do. However, as the largest company, British Airways would undoubtedly have wanted to impose its standards on KLM. Unfortunately, in the past the Dutch have not often shown a great sense of reality in accepting that size and power matter. The English are used to thinking politically, whereas the Dutch are more pragmatic.

Both cultures show a moderate individualism and are, therefore, less suited to manufacturing. The fate of the car industry in both countries speaks volumes. Dutch individualism knows its limitations in respect of decision making when it comes to an appeal for consensus. During any negotiations the British are stunned by the slow decision making of the Dutch; for them the need to confer is essential, even if top management is present.

The combination of emotional expression and the degree to which we deepen our relationships is the biggest hurdle between the English and the Dutch. This becomes clear from the following question.

Below is a description of four types of people. Please look at these descriptions and choose the one which you would like to resemble most.

1.   A person who is respected by others and constantly cares for the well-being of others. (Combination of neutral and diffuse orientations.)

2.   A person who is well liked by others and who takes their daily pleasures and concerns in their stride. (Combination of affective and specific orientations.)

3.   A person who is loved by others and who and who constantly cares for the personal well-being of those whom they love. (Combination of affective and diffuse orientations.)

4.   A person who is accepted by others and who dutifully goes about their daily business. (Combination of neutral and specific orientations.)

The Dutch mostly choose option 2; being nice is an emotion in a specific box. The English have a preference for option 1; respect is a diffuse, emotionally controlled orientation. Here we already see a significant difference between the English and the Dutch: The English, with their "stiff upper lip" are far more inclined to keep their emotions to themselves. Only through humor, hooliganism and alcohol do they show their true emotions. The Dutch are more specific and direct in expressing their emotions.

When I was at Shell a colleague of mine returned from a performance review. "For a moment I was scared that my English boss was going to fire me," he told me, "but he only said 'I suggest that you need to consider another job.'" He was mistakenly relieved. The English have what is called a "high context" style of communication. Since they know that privacy is incorporated in a relationship, they will use an indirect, often diplomatic, style of communicating. The English can say the same thing in different contexts in completely different ways. Generally, what the Dutch say is less dependent on the context. Where the English would say "you have an interesting personality," a Dutch person would say "you're an idiot, but don't take it personally." At Shell the Dutch were rarely invited to partake in diplomatic missions.

It is interesting that Dutch people often go to a meeting to discuss specific matters, yet the English find it strange when at the end of the meeting the question "So, what have we decided then, what are the action points?" is asked. The English usually keep the most important issues for after meetings.

This may well have been one of the biggest stumbling blocks in the negotiations. It seems to me that KLM conducted itself in a very Dutch manner. In respect of high context and diffuse relationships Italians are very similar to the English. However, there is one difference: The English are much subtler in expressing their frustrations than are the Italians. The latter will let you know immediately that you are wrong; the English will only tell you that you are being strangled when you are catching your last breath.

Finally, there is a difference in the way people acquire status. Although both the Dutch and the English are old monarchies, respecting professionalism and formal education, the Dutch have a preference for engineering and natural sciences, while the English tend to attach more importance to the reputation of the university you attended than the subject you studied. Nevertheless, the Dutch try to hide status differences. Bosses will roll up their sleeves and help their subordinates, if necessary. In public the English are much more hierarchal.

It is staggering to see the number of business class seats on one of BA's European flights. In contrast the very limited number of business seats on similar KLM flights is telling. Usually the Dutch are not fussy about looking down the aisle to the unattainable business class, as long as the curtain is drawn. The English are very much aware of the fact that you can only have a business class thanks to the existence of an economy class. Had the merger gone ahead, I would have had to wish KLM the very best of luck with seat allocation!

THE FRENCH CONNECTION

After all that, KLM began a love affair with Air France. Negotiations with the French are anything but easy, particularly for the Dutch who like to scrape the last bit of food from the plate.

For me, understanding French culture has been automatic: my mother is French (or, rather, she is from Paris); my father was born and raised in Amsterdam. We recently celebrated their fiftieth wedding anniversary. They are surprisingly happy, the main reason being that they have probably never understood each other. But what are the main differences between Dutch and French culture? Obviously, Protestant and Catholic backgrounds partly explain the significant differences. But there are also differences that can be traced back to the countries themselves.

Firstly, the Dutch have a tendency to strive for the ultimate and universal Truth, while the French prefer particularistic flexibility. Where the Dutch like to be motivated by reliability, the French are fond of the exception and the unique. There seems to be some misunderstanding about the individualism of the French. Geert Hofstede also describes the French as individualistic, but this probably says more about the quality of Hofstede's research than about the true nature of the French. As far back as I can remember, my family and I drove to the Atlantic coast from Amsterdam. It struck me that the French were all on vacation in August, and staying in quite large houses where the whole extended family, including grandparents and even distant cousins, were installed. They would all discuss French individualism, gathered around large tables, and always, always in big groups. If you have ever been on holiday with Club Med you will know that Fraternité often beats Liberté.

The French also love to challenge those in charge by *force majeure*. They believe that the differences in goals of various parties need to be fought out, while the Dutch tend to go for harmonious consensus. In addition the French believe that they need to control their environment, which is indicated by their drive to develop their own nuclear defense system, to speak French, or to understand other cultures. This internal control would have to be reconciled with the implicit need of the Dutch to keep on talking even after deals have been struck. It takes some time before you get to know the French but then they go the whole way. The Dutch don't understand their subtle diplomacy. They think they are rather unpredictable with their ever-changing opinions and rich use of language.

Finally the big French paradox is that they love to look back nostalgically to a very impressive past while at the same time trying to create a high-tech future. The French have not only produced the Arc de Triomphe and Versailles but also the TGV and the Pompidou Center. These seemingly opposing orientations are quickly resolved after an interview with an average Frenchman. He will whisper in your ear that there is no better guarantee for a *histoire grandiose* than to go for the high risk *grand project*. This was particularly clear during the socialist President Mitterand's last years. So, no budgetary constraints on a *grand project*. But the Frenchman will also warn you that a high-tech approach is not without risk: history has made it that way. And if you look at French history it goes from *Gloire* to *Catastrophe,* from Mitterand to Chirac. So KLM should have been more wary before making any assumptions.

THE FLEA IN THE EAR OF INTEL

Seven years ago, Martin Gillo, the Personnel Manager of Advanced Micro Devices (AMD) in Europe, approached Charles Hampden-Turner and me. AMD planned to open a new production facility in Dresden in former East Germany: "The only way to continue competing with Intel is to combine the best of German and American culture," stated Gillo. Intel was finding that the only way of keeping AMD at bay was continually to take them to court for "patent infringement." In the beginning of 2000 it became clear that the investment of 1.5 billion euros in the manufacturing of semiconductors was worth every penny: For the first time AMD had beaten Intel by managing to introduce the first gigahertz chip more than two days earlier than the chip giant. Is it true, then, that cultural integration has created something that rose above the capacity of a single culture?

After Charles and I had conducted our round of interviews in order to highlight the most important problem areas, we were not terribly optimistic. The cultural differences between Germans and Americans paled next to the animosity between East and West Germans. Both parties tried to form coalitions with the Americans just to spite each other. The Americans showed a slight preference for the East Germans as they tended to be good listeners and were more flexible. However, American–German misunderstandings were much more persistent.

The American semiconductor industry can attribute much of its success to the integration of individual creativity with teamwork, and to the successful completion of a long-term vision. AMD arrived in Dresden in typical American style: programs were executed in a stereotypical American manner; videos, workshops, and pep talks done the "Texan way" were combined in the pursuit of excellence. At the first interviews it became evident that this approach was highly amusing to the Germans: "All that exaggerated business about the importance of effective meetings and brainstorming. Let's just do our homework and everything will work out." About four dilemmas soon popped up. And Gillo, an energetic as well as sympathetic German, quickly saw that recouping the gigantic investment would be dependent on the creative power used in solving these dilemmas.

"Holistische weltanschauungen and analytical bottom lines." The Americans often complained about the slowness and lack of creativity of the Germans. The Germans in turn stated that the Americans were too premature, throwing even the most undeveloped ideas into brainstorming sessions; the Americans had immediately jumped to the conclusion that nothing would work out, as the Germans

showed no evidence of having brains to storm with. In our workshops, in which Germans as well as Americans participated, the reason for this became clear very quickly. The specific Americans can easily separate their ideas from the person. When criticized during a brainstorming session, they readily accept that "my idea was hacked to pieces, no problem, on with the next idea." The more diffuse Germans identify themselves with their ideas and will therefore not throw a half-baked one into a discussion. This would lead to loss of face: to the making public of something that is considered private. The solution seemed quite simple. Time-outs were built into each meeting, and the Germans blossomed. In private, it was easier to swap ideas (in German) and to criticize them too. These ideas were then collated, put down on Post-it notes and passed to the Americans. The Americans called this "train storming" because they had noticed that many German trains had private coupés. There was all-round astonishment at the resultant German creativity.

Always meetings but no preparation time. The Germans at AMD noticed that the American characteristic of "shooting from the hip" was a result of being unprepared for meetings. The Germans, in the eyes of the Americans, were too slow for this fast industry: "Aim, aim – oh, I forgot to shoot." The reconciliation of both cultures was found in a process where the Americans were asked to summarize the meetings and the Germans to set up the agenda on the basis of the minutes of the previous meeting. In a very implicit manner it came down to knowledge management. Americans were forced to share information and the Germans needed to become more specific.

Catch-up economy with market leadership. Dresden is the capital of Saxony and was the center of the former East German microchip industry. Many highly trained East German engineers were contracted by AMD. It soon became clear that education-wise they were on the same level as their West German counterparts but that their improvisation skills were much more developed. This is often seen in a catch-up economy where many capable people suddenly get access to the means that allow them to experiment and ultimately manufacture a product. The final result in AMD was clearly evident. The West Germans took care of the precise organizational structure in which the Americans could express their expertise and creativity. It was interesting to see the role that the former East Germans played: They were the oil that kept the machine running. At crucial moments they were able, via improvisation, to widen the critical path in the technical as well as the political area. Martin Gillo was convinced that AMD could never have been a threat to an organization such as Intel if the West Germans alone had been allied with the Americans.

A salient role in the integration process was the introduction of the "culture coach." We trained this person in the facilitating of multicultural teambuilding. In AMD, an organization somewhat reliant on meetings, this individual was responsible for guarding the cultural aspects of interactions. It was taken in turns, and the culture coaches played a crucial part in the enrichment of both the German and American cultures. You can bet your bottom dollar that in the future Intel will again feel someone on their heels.

KPN AND BELGACOM: A LARGE AND A SMALL LABYRINTH

Naturally, from my position as a cross-cultural adviser it was difficult to refrain from commenting on the possible joining of forces between the Dutch telecom company KPN and its Belgian equivalent Belgacom. In the event the negotiations failed. But had the two companies looked at the cultural side of the proposed integration?

Many books have been written in the Netherlands about the Belgian labyrinth, to which one Belgian commented: "The Netherlands is also a labyrinth, just one with very low trees." Dutch culture has also been extensively explored. It has not always been flatteringly described and it did not make me any more confident of a positive outcome of this merger.

Certainly, it was worthwhile predicting the typical Dutch–Belgian dilemmas and using the art of stereotyping to do so. This time, I have permitted myself to use the application of exaggeration a little bit more than I normally would: Belgians do in reality act more Belgian when in the company of the Dutch, and the Dutch are even more abrupt and specific in the company of Belgians than when among their own countrymen. What are the most important dilemmas in this cultural melting pot?

The Dutch and the Belgians have very different views on rules. The basically Protestant Dutch are accustomed to codifying their starting points within respected rules. There are even rules for exceptions – think of drugs, prostitution, or euthanasia. In the Netherlands you are not considered an idiot if you pay taxes; you try to find legal loopholes to soften the blow. The average (ex-) Catholic Belgian believes that you do not pay taxes unless the risk that you will be caught is too high.

This can definitely serve as a metaphor for a number of management dilemmas. On the one hand, you have the Dutch manager who wants to organize his activities around a depersonalized structure.

On the other hand, the Belgian director will want to spend most of his time in the further development of his business relationships. Most appointments are therefore made around lunchtime. A former Shell colleague told me that things went more smoothly after he hired a Belgian manager to run the office administration. In the new Shell Lab in Louvain-la-Neuve, the Belgian manager arranged for a number of crucial telephone lines in two days without one form having to be filled in. We had spent the previous four months trying to complete the many formalities with Belgacom, but he simply called his nephew, who in turn knew someone who could arrange it in a day. But don't make the mistake of thinking that there are fewer rules in Belgium. You just have to know someone who applies them. Reconciliation is certainly possible.

A second dilemma lies in the clash between the "direct" Dutch and the "closed" Belgian. If you know anything about the history of Belgium – the area has been occupied by others for most of the past 400 years – you will understand why they have such an affinity with tightly closed mussels and oysters. The specific Dutch culture often leads to an exaggerated segmentation of specializations and markets, whereas the diffuse, more reserved culture of the Belgians sometimes ends in a holistic pathology of unlimited networking. This dilemma can best be reconciled by exerting patience in building a relationship. After this is established, one can – in the right context – communicate very directly. And from experience, I know that the Belgians can beat the Dutch on this point.

Finally, there are dilemmas originating from different interpretations of hierarchy. The Dutch respect for opinions is close to the German inclination for professional expertise. You have to understand your business, and to express your opinion, and then be listened to as a colleague (the word "subordinate" leaves a bad taste in a Dutch mouth). But in contrast to a German, a Dutch person is not impressed by titles. That again is very different in Belgium. "Know who" is more important than "know how," and the symbolism of the job title is powerful. A Dutch manager of a Belgian bank subsidiary complained about the low level of motivation of his administrative staff. I advised him to take a close look at the job titles, which had been imported from the Netherlands: Departmental Secretary I, II and III. After the highest-ranking secretary had been promoted to Personal Assistant and two new titles introduced with a clear link to the level of the person for whom they worked, a more positive atmosphere quickly began to develop. And the manager wouldn't have been Dutch if he had not added "Not only is it in line with their culture, but best of all, it doesn't affect my budget." Belgians continue to be amazed about the desperate need for consensus that the Dutch seem addicted to. After listening carefully, a Belgian manager would rather make an individual decision.

The Dutch love the Belgians but do not always respect them; the Belgians often respect the Dutch but do not love them. It is not, perhaps, surprising that the merger failed.

TANGO IN CLOGS

It is very appealing to use the metaphor of marriage when talking about a merger or acquisition. One of our clients, an investment banker, often told me "We're in weddings, not in marriages."

It can also be reversed. During the ceremonies surrounding the wedding of the Dutch Prince Willem-Alexander to the Argentinean Maxima, I often thought about the merger of multicultural organizations. The National Wedding Gift was perfectly suited to this "mixed" marriage: the Orange Fund was set up to stimulate "the mutual relations between different cultures in the Netherlands."

However, the success of the Fund will depend on how its royal board members will fashion this merger. The multicultural marriage as well as the merger has a bad reputation. It frequently ends in divorce. If it goes well, and I know this from personal experience, it can be very worthwhile.

What could Willem-Alexander and Maxima do to make the best out of their multicultural union? A first glance shows that both cultures are accustomed to diversity. Dutch culture is highly influenced by its colonial past and Argentina consists mainly of immigrants from Italy, Spain, Germany, and European Jews. In both cultures women play a crucial role. Dutch women generally express themselves in a low-key manner, and dress more simply than their Argentinean equivalents, who laugh, wave, and only talk calmly when there is no other choice. Both Dutch and Argentinean women are very goal-oriented and do not refrain from conquering the man of their choice.

What tensions can we expect after the honeymoon phase is over? First of all, there is the Calvinist character of Dutch culture in which rules need to be respected even when they do not make sense. This bestows upon the Dutch their reliable but also their inflexible and moralistic image. Catholic Argentineans, like the French, prefer the exceptional and are characterized by flexibility and originality. Only 16 percent of the universalistic Dutch as opposed to 36 percent of the particularistic Argentineans said that they would lie to the judge in order to help a friend who had caused a car accident.

A second tension is created in the area of expressing emotions. Fifty-four percent of the Dutch agree with the statement that it is unprofessional to show your emotions openly, as against only 22 percent of the Argentineans. Nevertheless, Willem-Alexander has been able to follow the lead of the passionate Maxima. His enthusiasm during sporting events would have been highly appreciated in Argentina, despite the fact that his little dances had more in common with the Dutch clog dance than the Tango. Yet I expect some difficulties. Dutch society, full of cool know-it-alls, has already reprimanded the Prince a few times after his intuitive response to complex political issues. But he could well be able to learn from his wife how to use spontaneity as a strategic weapon.

The greatest challenge will be how an externally oriented Dutchman can work with an internally directed Argentinean woman. Look at the Tango. The man doesn't lead at all, even if it looks that way; the woman confidently shows where his feet have to go. In Argentina the man follows the woman wherever *she* goes. I suggest that Willem-Alexander had best become used to the concept of a Servant Leader. It is quite clear "at whose service" she is: that of diversity.

THERE ARE NO GRAY AREAS IN SWITZERLAND

The only thing that melts in Switzerland is cheese in a raclette or fondue. The logic of circumstance is unknown to the Swiss; their hearts often seem neither to be present nor capable of melting. I realized this some five years ago when the Hogeschule Sankt Gallen invited me to help them with a one-week workshop for a group of top managers from Alu-Suisse. The academics organizing the event insisted that my colleague and I *arrived* the evening before our one-day event to discuss details. And why not, knowing that this would alleviate the nerves of our Swiss hosts? But we were only expecting a twenty-minute meeting as our plane was due to touch down at 9.30 p.m. and we still had to drive an hour or so to our final destination. However, that would have given us more than enough time to finalize the last-minute preparations for a relatively standard program. All did not go according to plan, however: we simply walked from the terminal, through a deserted airport and over the pedestrian crossing – against a green light. Our resulting tickets for jaywalking were a great welcome to Switzerland.

We finally arrived at our destination at 11.00 p.m. and greeted the Herr Doctors who were ready with their questions. "Herr Dr. Trompenaars, let's start with the details of the program. When do you think we can start the coffee break?" "Between 10.00 a.m. and 10.15 a.m.," I answered. "But isn't fifteen minutes too short?" the Professor replied. "No," said I, "we start the break sometime between 10.00 a.m. and 10.15 a.m., it just depends on how the discussion unfolds." "How the discussion unfolds? We need to know exactly when the coffee needs to be served." The first misunderstanding was born. When we started to dispute the times of the lunch- and tea-breaks ("Are you sure, Dr. Trompenaars, we should only serve tea?") I couldn't resist making light of the situation by way of a little joke. "You know, Dr. Braun, in the event that this precision is typically Swiss, I should advise you to start manufacturing watches." "But Dr. Trompenaars, we have manufactured watches successfully for centuries." I tried to avoid eye contact with my colleague, who was on the verge of laughing out loud. Swiss people seem to strive for precision in almost everything, which doesn't serve them well in the cultivation of a sense of humor.

I had recently been skiing in Switzerland and had walked to a newsstand to read the headlines of a Dutch newspaper for the sporting news. The first page revealed everything I needed to know. When I put the paper back in the rack, the woman behind the little counter stopped me: "Sir, would you like to pay now, please?" I said I wasn't interested in the previous day's paper. She replied in a stern tone, explaining that I had to buy the paper because I had touched it. I couldn't think of anything else to say other than that I wasn't a chess player – if you touch a piece in a game of chess you have to move it – and walked away.

What is this universalistic tendency in the Swiss personality? And please don't tell me there are big differences amongst the Swiss. Whether you are in the German-, French-, or Italian-speaking parts, you will not find a greatly developed sensitivity for particular circumstances. In addition Trompenaars Hampden-Turner's database doesn't leave any trace of doubt. We confronted some 260 Swiss managers, well distributed over the diverse language groups, with the following dilemma:

> *You are a doctor for an insurance company. You examine a close friend who needs more insurance. You find that he is in pretty good shape, but you are doubtful about one or two minor points that are difficult to diagnose. What right does your friend have to expect you to shade the doubts in his favor, and would you help him?*

Seventy-five percent of the Swiss answered that their close friend had no right or some right and indicated that they wouldn't try to hide any dubious findings. Just compare that with 70 percent of the British, 63 percent of the French, 58 percent of the Dutch and 40 percent of the Egyptians. There is no nation that scores higher on this point than the Swiss.

During my Swiss vacation I suggested to my ski-mate that we should check whether the Swiss were aware of the typical Dutch phenomenon of the "grijs rijden" (a "gray ride," meaning that you deliberately pay less than an original ticket price). We both bought a ticket for SF 2.00 with a 50 percent child or seniority discount from a beautiful Swiss ticket machine. The ride was short – only 14 minutes and 32 seconds – but in no time we were looking straight into the eyes of a conductor. We showed our "gray tickets," which fortunately didn't give rise to any comment as to our actual ages, but we were asked for our discount cards, which we did not, of course, possess. "But gentlemen, you have an invalid ticket, so you owe me SF 2.00 each and a fine of SF 20 per person," was the response. We protested, because the ticket clearly indicated a "1/2" which could easily have been interpreted as a one-way ticket. "That could very well be the case, gentlemen, but the ticket machine clearly explains the type of ticket you needed," we were told.

After our workshop at the Hogeschule Sankt Gallen we were taken to the airport by Professor Dr. Braun, and I vividly remember this return journey. After we had carefully read the local warning notes on our hired chauffeur-driven car he stepped into the back seat with me and said "Dr. Trompenaars, the workshop has been very well received, partly because you have followed the schedule so precisely. Also, the unplanned presence of your colleague turned out to be a great success. May I propose that you add 50 percent of his normal fee to your invoice?" "No, Herr Professor, let's stick to our original agreement," I replied. After a passionate discussion for the sake of politeness I tried to break the ice with "You should think about developing financial services in Switzerland." He winked at me and smiled. I think the Swiss should now join the euro. And the same holds true for the membership of the UN. But the country also needs a more developed sense of humor.

CHAPTER 4

People

The role of human resource managers has changed dramatically over recent years and so, of course, have the dilemmas they face. Back in the nineteenth century the individual was seen in terms of their physical abilities; you employed a pair of hands. It was irritating that these had a person on the other end – though in fact it was probably not even recognized that there was a real person present. This new paradigm, stemming from the industrial revolution, stipulated that management had to tell people what to do. With the coming of "shareholder value," humans were still seen as replaceable resources.

Today we see people as individuals with a whole variety of needs. Management now needs to create a customized workplace in which there is a synergistic balance between organizational and individual stakes. In this new world the basis of authority has become the way we effectively reconcile dilemmas. In this chapter it will become apparent that the systems and processes of HR gradually evolve into an instrumental approach to reconciling the dilemmas of management.

FROM BALANCED TO INTEGRATED SCORECARDS

Almost everything in our work environment has changed in recent years, and so has the role of HR managers. The nature of the dilemmas they face has changed too. Can you imagine HR managers advising their hunter-gatherer ancestors how to capture more animals by motivating people more effectively?

Hamid Bouchikhi and John Kimberly have noted that in nineteenth-century thinking a person was seen in terms of either muscle or energy. Management decided what their reactive[1] employees would do. The twentieth century changed the employee into a subordinate with a hierarchy of needs (and, I would add, a need for hierarchy). In the present century we see the development of autonomous and reflective individuals. They have a full set of needs, both internal and external to the organization. Power is diffuse and shared. Management needs to co-create a "customized workplace." A recent article in the *Financial Times* (Bouchikhi and Kimberly, 2001) pointed this out: "In contrast with traditional management, where structures and systems are derived from a pre-defined strategy, the design of the customized workplace will seek to balance what matters for the company (its strategy) and what matters for the individuals (their life strategies)." In fact, management and employees interactively decide and execute this. In this world some conflict is a normal part of life and reconciling dilemmas is the source of most authority. This is amplified even more by the continuous process of globalization. What has the response of HR professionals been?

In the nineteenth century HR practices were unknown, but in the early twentieth century we see an increasingly active HR profession. In *Organizational Capability* David Ulrich has argued that the concepts behind HR have evolved over millennia, but became more structured during the 1930s when companies set up industrial relations departments. In the 1940s selection tools began to be more

---

1   Russ Ackoff distinguishes inactive, reactive, proactive, and interactive as the main distinguishable approaches.

aggressively developed, as did systems for evaluating jobs. Many of these systems were developed to meet the needs of the American army (HAY, etc.). The 1950s and 1970s shifted attention to legal issues; in addition, compensation systems began to emerge with "pay for performance" and the like. The 1980s moved the agenda further towards thinking about systems rather than people. These HR systems became integrated and aligned with strategy. However, with the arrival of one of the most over-rated concepts, the well-known shareholder value, humans beings were still only seen as replaceable resources. To add continued value, HR has been forced to become more than a partner: It has become a player, contributing to the creation of the customized workplace.

The systems and processes of HR are adapting slowly but surely to the world of dilemmas created by this customized workplace and also by globalization. Values must be integrated into this new paradigm.

One of the most striking of all approaches enabling HR professionals and management to integrate value, rather than to add it, is the Balanced Scorecard developed by Robert Kaplan and David Norton. Recognizing some of the weaknesses and vagueness of previous measurement approaches, their scorecard provides a clearer prescription as to what management should measure to "balance" the dominant financial perspective of the late eighties and early nineties. Kaplan and Norton summarize the rationale for the Balanced Scorecard as follows:

> The balanced scorecard retains traditional financial measures. But financial measures tell the story of past events, an adequate story for industrial-age companies for which investments in

long-term capabilities and customer relationships were not critical for success. These financial measures are inadequate, however, for guiding and evaluating the journey that information-age companies must make to create future value through investment in customers, suppliers, employees, processes, technology, and innovation.

The balanced scorecard suggests that we view the organization from four perspectives, and that we develop metrics, collect data, and

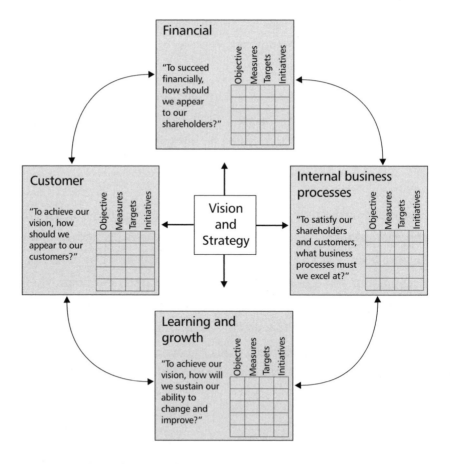

Figure 4.1 The organization from four perspectives.

Source: http:/www. balancedscorecard.org/basics/bsc1.html.

analyze it relative to each of these perspectives, as shown in Figure 4.1

The learning and growth perspective

This perspective includes employee training and corporate cultural attitudes related to both individual and corporate self-improvement. In a knowledge organization, people – the foremost repository of knowledge – are the main resource. In the current climate of rapid technological change, it is becoming necessary for knowledge workers to be in a continuous learning mode. Measurements can be put into place to guide managers in focusing training approaches where they can help the most. In any case, learning and growth constitute the essential foundation for success of any knowledge-worker organization. Kaplan and Norton emphasize that "learning" is more than "training." It also includes things like mentors and tutors within the organization, as well as the ease of communication among workers that allows them to readily obtain help with a problem when it is needed.

The business process perspective

This perspective refers to internal business processes. Measurements based on this perspective allow managers to know how well their business is doing, and whether its products and services conform to customer requirements (the mission). These metrics have to be carefully designed by those who know these processes most intimately – people within the organization.

The customer perspective

Recent management philosophy has shown an increasing realization of the importance of customer focus and customer satisfaction in any business. These are leading indicators: If customers are not satisfied, they will eventually find other suppliers who will meet their needs. Poor performance from this perspective is thus a leading indicator of future decline, even though the current financial picture may look good.

The financial perspective

Kaplan and Norton do not disregard the traditional need for financial data. Timely and accurate funding data will always be a priority, and managers will do whatever is necessary to provide it. In fact, there is often more than enough handling and processing of financial data. With the implementation of a corporate database, it is hoped that more of the processing can be centralized and automated. But the point is that the current emphasis on financials leads to an unbalanced situation with regard to other perspectives.

The balanced scorecard is a management system (and not purely a measurement system) that enables organizations to clarify their vision and strategy and translate them into action. It provides feedback around both the internal business processes and external outcomes in order to continuously improve strategic performance and results. When fully deployed, the balanced scorecard transforms strategic planning from an academic exercise into the nerve center of an enterprise.

In reality, the way this system is often used shows clearly that it is a transitional process between paradigms. The word "balance" symbolizes this, because when one perspective goes up the other must go down. That is often necessary when you strongly believe that the purely short-term financial perspective, well catered for by the shareholder philosophy, is at the cost of longer-term future perspectives. In order to make this management system more effective in the new paradigm of the customized workplace, we would like to see an Integrated Scorecard.

We will need to reconcile the two major cultural dilemmas that underlie the original scorecard –the Past (Financial) and the Future (Learning and Growth) Perspective dilemma and the Internal (Business Process) and the External (Customer) Perspective dilemma. The best support for the vision and strategy of the organization is found not in how past financial performance could be balanced with future growth but how it can be reconciled with it: For example, it could be that certain financial surpluses were reserved for the following year's learning budgets. I have found a Finnish organization, Partek, doing this in a consistent way.

In addition we need to improve the internal processes through the involvement of (external) customers. Co-development programs, where suppliers align strategically with their clients are a great example. Take Applied Materials, one of the main suppliers of machines producing microchips. Their survival is completely dependent on co-developing systems with AMD and Intel.

This is quite different from balance. It supposes that having high scores in each of the four perspectives and adding them up do not add value. That needs integration of past and future, internal and external values.

MOMENTS OF TRUTH

Returning from Japan recently I realized once more how differently various cultures perceive customer service. In a Japanese restaurant,

the waiters asked at exactly the right moment if we still had sufficient sake left, or if the soy sauce still contained enough wasabi. It
seemed as if they were counting each bite and each sip, because they
were literally "just in time." What a contrast this forms with Dutch
service levels, where avoiding eye contact with the customer at crucial moments has been elevated to a national sport. You get excellent
service when you don't need it, and no service when you do: If my
empty glass needs to be refilled from the wine bottle in the ice
bucket (curiously enough my wife's glass remains in a permanent
state of fullness), there's no sign of a waiter anywhere.

On the other hand, you don't want exaggeration either, as I have
often experienced in American shops. There the door has barely
closed before you are almost assaulted by employees asking you
what you need and how they can help you. In such a situation, I prefer being ignored. The art is to offer assistance at the right moment,
something – following Jan Carlzon – I would describe as a "moment
of truth."

The expectation patterns about service are clearly influenced by
one's own culture. I was shocked to read in *The Times* recently that
Asian banks carried over $2,000 billions of bad loans in their books.
Now that I call customer service, all be it in rather a pathological
form, but I don't entirely understand their logic of "the client is
always first." A Japanese bank will not drop a formerly solid client
at the first small crisis; they will have built up a diffuse relationship
that goes far beyond mere financial mutual understanding. The
many dinners the banker and the client will have shared in Tokyo
mean that the bank cannot run the risk of loosing face, and that
means continuing funding. These kinds of relationships develop in

Japan on a national scale. One can only guess at the consequences after ten years of a vacillating economy.

This is in strong contrast to what the – rather more liquid – European banks are offering: an impressive portfolio of products and services, all yours to choose from. But that applies only until the moment you really need them. Five years ago, I urgently needed some money to buy out a partner of my firm. The bank asked me what my financial background was and what I earned. I told them I had nothing substantial in terms of personal wealth and that, if I earned enough, I would not be borrowing from them. At that moment, I realized that the essence of Dutch banking is that they will only lend you money when you already have it. In Japan there is a service mentality that has outgrown normal limits without any checks and balances, whereas in more specific cultures the system breaks down when losing sight of the diffuse aspect of relationships.

The answer to this service dilemma can be found in moments of truth: "Moments" are specific, while "truth" is diffuse. Often, the solution cannot be found at the level that these dilemmas occur. Airline companies, for example, have started to identify where they want to go deep, and where not. Singapore Airlines and Virgin are excellent examples of this. They know exactly what it takes to please the client, without compromising security. It is incredible what they will do if you miss a connection, or have lost a piece of luggage. And that is what their customers want.

Now, if my Dutch bank should start to look where it should go deep, it would definitely be able to withstand any global competition. Were that to happen, I would not be obliged to answer any more questions from foreigners about my opinion on Dutch customer service with "It would be an excellent idea!"

CO-OPETITION: COMPETE FOR THE BEST COOPERATION

In the early years of the century we are seeing an increasing number of companies opting for an increase in variable pay. Philips, the electronics giant, even considered breaking their important Collective Labor Agreement to be able to do so in the year 2000. The fight between a higher fixed income against lower variable income and vice versa seems to be insurmountable.

Appraisal and reward systems seemed to attract lots of attention in the management literature of the last century. "How can I best motivate and retain my top people, and how can I effectively provide feedback on their performance?" were frequently raised questions. It is striking just how many research findings have shown that money is not the main motivating factor at all: Rather it is a so-called "dissatisfier." Experience shows that employees only feel good for a short while about their expected bonuses; they quickly become used to them and then move on to reach for the next illusion. This can hardly be compared to the negative feelings and demotivating effect that can arise if a financial reward is below expectations. Recovering from this blow, even to the point of average motivation, can take months. It is interesting that human nature is so attracted to money. Money, however, can play a positive role as a symbol of much deeper values. The relative feeling of "I have earned more than my colleague" seems to be more important than the absolute high point of the bonus. The situation in the new economy, where financial consultants and e-commerce staff receive variable rewards of 60–90 percent, is quite hilarious: If you look at the relationship between the level of their workmanship and the growth of turnover or profitability, the question really needs to be raised of just how large their contribution actually is.

Twenty-year-old research from Northwestern University reveals that the quality of management is only responsible for 10 percent of company results. If you look at the relationship between the price of crude oil and the results of oil companies and you see the results of financial institutions, the Wall Street, or FT Index then I think that the results of this research are still valid. Even with mediocre management and large losses you can acquire unbelievable income, and pat yourself on the back too.

A second assumption of most reward systems is that one has to motivate the individual. I met an American HR manager who claimed that his company had developed a very interesting system of performance reward, based on 50 percent variable pay, including options that would only materialize after three years of active service. Short- and long-term thinking were reconciled in this approach and people seemed to be highly motivated by the belief that their performance had a direct effect on the functioning of the organization as a whole. He had to admit, however, that this approach had met with much resistance in Europe and Asia. In Europe mainly because of tax constraints, but in Asia no clear reason could be provided. "Could it be culture?" he asked me.

Indeed, and the solution is quite straightforward. If you are in America, you retain the individual reward system. In Asia you can motivate people by a team reward structure. In Europe you do everything to avoid paying tax. But there is a hidden problem. This decentralized approach works very well for a multinational organization. If, however, you grow into a transnational firm, characterized by many multicultural teams in which all sorts of different people with different motivations are united, the reward system needs to be adapted accordingly.

In the internationalization process a new logic is necessary regarding the way we think about management. There are some options that do not work well. The first one is to train all employees to take responsibility for their own creativity. This is called the "individual-ization of society" on a collective level. The problem remains, as the individualized human being is not keen on sharing information.

With the reward system detailed above there is an option to choose to reward people for team spirit. People from Japan excel at this, but it often leads to collective mediocrity. The worst is the compromise; namely rewarding the small team. Both the individualist and the team player feel demotivated. But what is the alternative?

Consider the discussion of reward systems in the US semiconductor industry. Is it not amazing that due to Asian effectiveness in the eighties, a complete industry on the brink of collapse made an unprecedented comeback, thanks to agreements made within the cooperative institution of Sematech? The American Ministry of Defence founded Sematech so that American chip manufacturers and their suppliers could cooperate in order to better compete with their Asian rivals. A classic example of "co-opetition: cooperate to compete." You also find this spirit back in the organizations them-selves, as in Intel, AMD, and National Semiconductor, all aimed at creative individuals forming teams that surpass the individual. These organizations have managed to do just that; look at the results.

At the end of the 1980s we tried similar things at Shell in Amsterdam. An experiment with the 2000 staff in the research and development division was based on the joining together of creative individual researchers of different nationalities. In the space of a year, we evenly distributed 20 percent variable pay over individual and team bonuses. The individual bonus was given to the person chosen by the team as the best team player. The team bonus went to the team that excelled in supporting individual creativity. The Shell researchers from Amsterdam competed for the best cooperation in teams, and they worked together in order to compete better.

Another recent example concerns the advice that the consultant Gallway gave to IBM's sales force. Instead of those who sold the most personal computers receiving a bonus, which placed stress on the sales person and the client, Gallway suggested an alternative. Every quarter sales people made a presentation of what they had learned from their customers, and collected the bonus. Sales figures rose by 25 percent, the clients were satisfied, and information was exchanged between the sales people. This, again, is co-opetition: competing for the cooperation with the client. The best sales staff, we later learned, were those who learned most from their clients.

NEW DILEMMAS IN THE WAR FOR TALENT

At the end of the last century McKinsey and Drucker introduced the concept of the "War for Talent." As the most important factor in competition shifted from scarce capital and product to the talent of workers, the major question became "How can employers attract and retain scarce talent for their organizations?"

I don't believe that mature organizations have ever thought any differently about the importance of recruiting gifted employees. However, the values with which organizations have tried to entice these scarce human resources are very different now.

I can still remember which values attracted me to Shell twenty years ago. First and foremost was the "name." Shell, Heineken, and Unilever were at the top of the list as the most attractive companies: Shell because of its international reputation and high quality jobs, Heineken because of the attractiveness of the product and Unilever for the kind of organization it was. Then my father would add "Working for any of those three will ensure you a job for life."

It is no coincidence that in the late 1990s there was a shift in thinking about how to recruit and retain young talent. The employment market was tight. The Internet boom was approaching its a highest point. Many young people thought there was a direct connection between their limitless talent and the results of their own start-up companies. This was particularly the case within the financial services and high-tech fields. Although the heyday for this generation, accustomed to making a quick buck, is slowing down, the tension between the demand and the supply of well-educated and talented personnel has not diminished.

Not only has the demand for quality employees changed in terms of numbers, but also in terms of profile. An analysis of our database shows that the younger generation – from 20–30 years of age – have become more directed in the last few years. They dare to express their emotions more, and they feel better working in teams. Moreover, it appears that the younger, high-potential employees focus on the short-term, and have a greater confidence in their own individual abilities. Their preference has shifted from the task-oriented

"Guided Missile" to the person-oriented "Incubator" work environment. In this respect, the dot.com organizations appear to have responded particularly well.

These days, what makes a large organization attractive to a young, ambitious, and talented employee? On the demand side, organizations of the old economy are discovering that it is increasingly difficult to find good candidates. It is apparent that established organizations like Shell, Heineken, and Unilever must make an enormous effort to catch up with the attractiveness of younger businesses. There is a tension between the image of these companies and the ideals that young, talented people have in their minds. The power-oriented "Family" culture and the role-oriented hierarchical structures of the so-called "Eiffel Tower" culture still dominate these large companies in both perception and reality. The big players realize this and are doing their best to change.

If you browse the website that Shell uses to recruit young academics, you see the dilemmas that arise from the tension between corporate image and personal vision. Shell is looking for people who are global, innovative, team players; people who think in terms of diversity, who want to learn, and who value freedom of choice. At face value this doesn't look culturally sensitive. But global thinking doesn't seem so attractive to young people any more. Young, talented graduates prefer to work locally. Therefore, Shell also recruits people who want to choose between regions, divisions, and functions.

There seems to be a dilemma between global (one world) thinking and thinking that values diversity (many realities). Shell invites people who believe in the equal treatment of men and women, and asks people from all different ethnic backgrounds to develop into citizens of the world. In the same way, you can imagine the dilemmas that arise between being oriented towards teamwork (stability/ tradition) and being oriented towards innovation. The Japanese experience demonstrates that it is not easy to reconcile both.

Apart from the dilemmas between Shell's espoused orientations, there are also dilemmas adhering to the image of a large organization and doubt as to whether these orientations can be put into practice. However, it is clear that ultimately only those organizations that reconcile these dilemmas will remain attractive in the employment market. There are some good examples of this. The American semiconductor industry has shown that, by creatively reconciling teamwork and individual creativity, you can become an unbeatable player in your sector. Transnational organizations such as Nokia and Applied Materials show how to keep excellent talent by globalizing diversity.

I would very much like to belong to an organization where free choice, deep learning opportunities, image, and reality have all been reconciled. There is still a lot of work to do if we want to win the war for talent.

THE LEARNING ORGANIZATION – OR, RATHER, HOW TO ORGANIZE LEARNING

Professional trainers and consultants are increasingly confronted with questions from clients of how their knowledge can be embedded into the company's long-term learning processes, or of how they can help the client's organization build and sustain "cultures of learning," "cultures of continuous development," and "cultures that embrace change and diversity."

Many educational programs in our schools, universities, and within our organizations are based on presenting codified knowledge, which is dumped on the heads of the students. And the teachers, who have developed or captured this knowledge, fulfil their roles as "knowledge dumpers" with great gusto. Just look at the way that many classrooms and even professional conference centers are designed. The podium (preferably in an elevated position) stands out in great contrast to the uncomfortable chairs that are huddled behind folding tables in the rest of the room.

The greatly respected Russ Ackoff used to cite a telling story which reveals this mindset (Ackoff, 1987). A teacher asked his students "How can you connect nine dots, drawn on a piece of paper in a square of three lines with three dots each, using four straight lines – without lifting your pen from the paper?" The students were given two days to think about the answer. At the end of the two days, only two students had a solution. (Those of you who have attempted this exercise may remember that you need to go outside the imaginary square.) One successful student gave the answer that one line would suffice if you folded the paper in such a way that the three lines of three dots met, and subsequently drew your line. This is one interesting solution but the teacher reacted with obvious irritation indignantly asking if the students had been told that they could fold the paper, and thereby punishing the successful student for her original contribution. Unfortunately, this kind of scenario is far too common.

In order to break out from of the imaginary square of the traditional principles of learning and to build a true learning organization, I distinguish a certain number of dilemmas that characterize an alternative learning process.

Firstly, there is the dilemma of a universal team style versus a diversity of learning styles. In a recent research project within Heineken we found that their employees' team styles differed more significantly than their cultural backgrounds. As a business, how can you cope with this if you need to develop and apply globally consistent learning programs? One suggestion is to globally apply the learning cycle as developed and described by David Kolb in his book *Experiential Learning*.

Kolb's cycle includes four stages: experiencing, reflecting, conceptualizing, and planning and generalizing. He suggests that each culture needs to go through the full cycle. However, in the USA the case study or simulation seems to be the most effective starting point, whereas in France, a kick-off with theories and conceptualizations leads to better results because they tend to say "I see what happens in practice, but first prove to me that it will work in theory." By choosing a particular approach, a learning organization can take better advantage of the diversity of its members. In this way, you can see that within a learning organization the learning cycle can be universalized while the points of departure within the cycle are culturally dependent. And what about universal, supply-driven training curricula versus particularistic, demand-driven, ad-hoc sessions?

A second dilemma that needs to be reconciled is that of the value of individual versus group learning. Many learning processes focus solely on the individual. The individual completes tests and receives feedback. Obviously, the learning organization is dependent on the knowledge of individuals, but the organization will only increase its effectiveness when the individual is inspired by a surrounding group. One way of achieving this might be to have the individual sales person or researcher compete for the best cooperation with the customer or fellow-researchers. You could also have an approach aimed rather at stimulating the cooperation between colleagues to share best practices in such a way that everyone learns from each other. This reconciliation can be described as "cooperative competitive learning" – you raise the best ideas in a competitive context in order to have the entire organization cooperate around the best practices. I remember, during my time at Shell, being sent on creativity training. It was very enlightening. The next Monday I was ready to practice some of the interesting techniques I had learned on my colleagues. It was as if I had landed from Mars; the result was deeply disappointing. No, you have to frame individual learning in a group context. A learning organization is also a changing one, in which you can only change individually if the organization around you changes in parallel, and I mean here changes in a sustainable way. In other words, while individuals are trying to implement cultures of continuous development, which takes time and patience, their organizations can deal at the same time with a series of pressures that fly in the face of their original desire (cost pressures, urgent need to deliver value to the customer today, etc.).

A third dilemma which arises when challenging traditional learning processes is that between action and reflection. For a long time it has been recognized that purely cognitive learning or "reflection" results in limited learning. It creates the Ivory Tower scientist. To counter this, many organizations go for "action learning," as can be witnessed by the increased popularity of the case study approach in universities. But action learning also has some constraints. Take the example of a Harvard student in his first well-paid job, struggling with a particular problem. The only thing he could say to his boss, as an excuse, was that he had never worked on this kind of case before. The particular weakness and limitation of action learning programs is that they are too often disconnected from any reflection on the overall context of the individual problems the organization is facing. A learning organization can benefit by having "action learning" as a principle, where action is undertaken on specific issues, and with workshops then used to share knowledge and reflection, but only in order to move into action once more – this time in a more informed and effective way.

The tensions I have mentioned can all serve as challenges in creating learning organizations. But they can also definitely bring about real change if reconciled, which can result in companies' becoming, for example, more diversity-minded or more global. In all these dilemmas, one discovers an organizational principle that is based on the idea of integration. One will have to leave the Cartesian and deductive model behind, and to bring a synthesis of the dilemmas that form the basis of learning.

THE SOUND OF ONE HAND CLAPPING

I clearly remember a cartoon in which a huge HR manager, sporting a moustache, cigar and a tartan jacket is interviewing a tiny candidate with the same style of jacket, a little moustache and a cigarette. The HR manager is saying "Yes, in view of what you have told us, I think you would be a very good candidate for the vacancy."

Don't we all recognize this? Don't we all look for the same characteristics that we ourselves have, consciously or unconsciously? Indeed, recruitment is often a sophisticated way of cloning. This is the major reason why professionals have sought to develop tools to assess the main traits of a candidate in a more rigorous and objective manner. Particularly well known is the MBTI tool developed by Myers-Briggs. This Myers-Briggs Type Indicator has probably been the most widely used personality inventory in history. HR professionals have seized on it in order to help their clients make important business, career, or personal decisions. Last year alone, two million people gained insights into themselves and the people they interact with on a daily basis by completing the MBTI.

The MBTI is an explicit application of the tacit genius of Carl Jung. One of Jung's most significant findings was the realization that, by understanding the way we process information, we can gain insights into why we act and feel the way we do. In particular he determined that, in order to better understand ourselves, we first need to understand the way we perceive, and then act upon, information. Derived from Jung's insights, the MBTI distinguishes four basic psychological processes that can each be plotted on a bi-polar scale.

The first scale describes where you tend to focus your attention and from where you get your energy. On the one extreme you have *Extroversion*, where the source of energy comes from the outside world. *Introversion*, at the other extreme, is where one's power derives from within oneself. A second scale describes how one gathers information. This distinguishes *Sensing* – when information is captured in a literal and concrete sense – and *Intuition*, when we give meaning to our data by putting it in a larger context. The way we judge information, and take decisions based upon how we perceive it, is captured in a third scale. Those who take decisions on the basis of logic and ratio can be spoken of as having a preference for *Thinking*. In contrast, when one prefers to take decisions on the basis of values or things one stands for, we speak of a dominant *Feeling* preference. The final scale describes a preference for how one orients oneself to the outside world and how one organizes information. On one extreme there is a dominance of *Perceiving* information, preferring flexibility and spontaneity. At the other extreme is *Judging*, for those who have a preference for organizing things in an orderly and disciplined manner.

Research has sought to correlate these scales with different job categories and functions. There is evidence to suggest which dominant type best fits a marketing role and which type is found most often among successful managers. With the internationalization of business we are suddenly confronted with some interesting dilemmas which challenge this principle.

The type ESTJ – Extroverting, Sensing, Thinking, Judging – occurs relatively frequently and may have some success in North America. There is other evidence that the type INFP – Introversion, Intuition, Feeling, Perceiving – is more often found amongst managers in Latin cultures. When seeking to apply the MBTI typology, or indeed any other associative model, in an international context we find that accretion to the extremities of each scale is constraining. Take this analogy: Despite professional psychologists discussing preference with reference to the dominance of our right or left hand when writing, it remains a poor solution. Both could be used, but one is usually dominant. Whilst this model can be applied to explain individual writing, it hardly helps you when you're applauding. While applauding it doesn't matter which hand is dominant; success depends on the coordination between both. Although MBTI profes-sionals do talk about combining the variety of preferences in teams and organizations, one cannot derive this approach from the MBTI tool, as it is based on forced-choice bi-model questions. Our own research shows that international leaders are more effective when able to integrate seemingly opposing values on a higher level.

Let's apply this thinking to the Myers-Briggs scales. To test the pref-erence for Thinking or Feeling the following question is asked:

When I make a decision I think it is most important:
(a)   *To test the opinions of others*
(b)   *To be decisive*

How the respondent answers this question gives insight if the domi-nant culture in which it is applied prefers decisiveness or being consulted (as in the original mode for which MBTI was developed). But in a multicultural environment one finds people with different opinions. The decisive leader will go broke on the fact that many want to go for consensus. Conversely, the sensitive leader will not succeed because of an apparent lack of decisiveness. The addition of two alternative options provides a means of evaluating the effective-ness of a leader in a multicultural group:

(c)   *To be decisive through continuously testing the opinions of others*
(d)   *To test the opinions of others by showing decisiveness*

A second example focuses on the preference between Judging and Perceiving:

While tackling an issue I would rather work:

(a)   *In a structured and organized way*

(b)   *Flexibly, with any necessary improvisation*

In Germany there is a tendency to score higher on (a) while (b) would appeal more to the French. But would one not be better off in a group of Germans and Latins when issues are approached in:

(c)   *A structured way in order to stimulate improvisation within certain boundaries*

(d)   *With the necessary improvisation, but trying to develop the best procedures and organization*

Our objections to applying MBTI across international boundaries may be explained by our own over-developed extreme profiles. But still we insist that the leader of today can flourish in diversity by combining seemingly opposing orientations. No one has ever measured anything like that.

And clapping with one hand makes little noise.

THE NECESSARY ROLES OF A SUCCESSFUL TEAM

The anthropologist Margaret Mead once said "Small groups have changed the world. Indeed nothing else ever has." The qualities of a leader, of the team and the interaction between both are the most important criteria making or breaking the success of an organization. On both subjects many books are written, and rightly so.

For me the most original thinker on management teams is the British author and consultant Meredith Belbin. In his first book, *Team Roles at Work,* he described how the Apollo team of highly talented people achieved significantly less than a second team made up of very much less gifted people, but who cooperated infinitely better. For Belbin an effective team is a group of people who aim for a shared goal, and therefore go through a number of phases. After 40 years of research he concludes that the effectiveness of a team is dependent on the fulfilment of eight complementary roles. They don't have to be there proportionally; nor need one individual play each of the roles since one person can incorporate different ones.

In the first phase of the definition of the task Belbin distinguishes the roles of the Shaper and the Chairman. Shapers are extrovert goal-getters who integrate different aspects of relevant activities into a coherent whole. They will frequently test the ineffectiveness of a team in a very impatient way. On the contrary, Chairmen comple-ment Shapers in the first phase by their rest and patience, but simultaneously appreciate all potential contributions and meld them together in the context of a very strictly managed set of goals.

In the second phase of generating ideas and gaining information, two new roles are dominant. First is the unorthodox Plant, generat-ing creative ideas. Plants are loaded with imagination and creativity and generate one proposal after the other. Just what the Plants con-tribute in terms of content, the Resource Investigators add to the level of process. They will sell ideas enthusiastically and will be able to negotiate extra budgets from management.

In the third phase there is a need for planning and collection of resources. Here the specialized roles of the Team Worker and the Company Worker are crucial. Team Workers are emotionally intelli-gent people with great social skills, reconciling the conflicts in the team and giving the necessary support, even if it means making the coffee. Company Workers translate the ideas into concrete tasks and are also willing to execute them personally. They have analytical minds and love organizing.

Finally, in the fourth phase, tasks need to be critically analyzed and completed. Here is where the Monitor Evaluator and the Completer/Finisher come in. The first role takes care of distant and mild criticisms, critically evaluating problem analyses. Completer/Finishers are the conscientious and anxious perfectionists, assuring in a professional way that the team finishes all its tasks.

What I mostly appreciate in the Belbin model are the implicit values that are associated with the diverse roles. In most theories about team roles many characteristics of the differing roles are summed up as though they were stable and as if they could independently guarantee a certain continuity. In reality, however, the effectiveness of a team is fully dependent on how it takes advantage of the differences in roles, in which the dynamic of complimentarity is essential. In particular, in the transitions between each of the four phases the differences between the roles become even clearer, and the reconciliation of the different orientations becomes essential.

For example, take the tension between the relaxed but task-oriented Chairman and the opportunistic Resource Investigator who continuously looks for new possibilities. A team will be able to function effectively when the issues that the Resource Investigator introduces from the outside can be reconciled with the more inwardly directed goals of the Chairman.

A second dilemma that needs to be resolved is the tension between the deviating Plant and the mediating Team Worker. Quite frequently, a new idea from a Plant initiates a fight between deviation and consensus. However, if some members of the team support the idea, there is nothing that can stop them and the team will flourish.

A third field of tension is often found between the Company Worker and the Completer/Finisher. The first believes in the success of hard work; the latter believes in a focus on details. This can result in many tensions that can be relieved if the first can convince the Completer that no details are being overlooked.

The last dilemma is created between the skeptical view of the Evaluator and the more optimistic approach of the action-oriented Shaper, who is often irritated by the amount of time that the process of evaluation and discussion is costing. The Shaper furthermore needs to transfer the apparent lack of inspiration and motivational image of the cool calculator into passionate enthusiasm. As with all these types of dilemmas, reconciliation can lead to mold-breaking new solutions and tilt the team towards higher levels.

The creation of wealth is often created by complimentarity of roles within a society and its organizations. The success of a team is dependent on whether all the roles are played by one or more of its members. This gives us a deeper meaning of the concept of diversity. The identification of these roles is only the beginning. The role of a leader needs to be particularly aimed at reconciling the crucial dilemmas created between the team roles, and in this way organizing the relationship between the roles. In such a way, the basic requirements for the team's success are well planted and ready to grow.

CHAPTER 5

Functions

The increasing internationalization of business has caused many functional disciplines to redefine and rethink their very essence. HR professionals, for example, face one dilemma after another. Similarly, marketing managers are becoming increasingly aware that the outcome of the global/local fight has become vital to their own survival, and the essential relationship between R&D and marketing is one of the most important and sensitive ones in business. Business literature has very much focused on cultural issues like national and organizational cultures; functional cultures and their effects on cross-functional relationships are almost forgotten. But they are also important…

DILEMMAS OF INTERNATIONAL HUMAN RESOURCE MANAGEMENT

The further internalization of business causes HR professionals to face increasingly bigger dilemmas. Human resource managers are increasingly coming to realize the limitations of an Anglo-Saxon bias as the main point of departure for personnel policy and instruments formulated in London and New York.

Take, for example, the HAY performance system, which supposes a separation between function and person; in a Latin environment that is impossible. Then what about the Japanese opinion of a reward system based on the individual performance of competing colleagues? Popular "assessment center" recruiting techniques are perceived by Greeks as an obnoxious game invented by desperate business school professors. And all of that is without even considering the criteria on which candidates are judged during recruitment and job appraisal processes.

In multi-local organizations there is no problem at all. Such organizations can follow a decentralized approach, so that in Japan a group reward scheme dominates and in France a graphological test is used when considering the quality of young graduates. However, transnational organizations face the problem that many activities take place in multicultural teams, and this can lead to big dilemmas for effective HR people. Various "unofficial" solutions have been attempted: I have coached French management teams that have first promoted a person and then described the function in order to satisfy centrally imposed function evaluation requirements, and I have observed groups of Asian employees in an American company hand their individual bonuses to their boss, and request that he look after the distribution within the team.

There is an alternative. Approximately five years ago Motorola introduced an interesting process in order to stimulate a dialogue between bosses and their subordinates under the title "Individual Dignity Entitlement." A number of times a year a dialogue unfolds around six important questions such as "Is the work you do meaningful?" and "Do you have enough resources to fulfill your tasks?" Yes or no are the only possible answers. When the answer is "yes" there is hardly any dialogue, but when the answer is "no" there must be a discussion on how to ensure that the answer is in the affirmative at the next interview.

This system launched by Christopher Galvin, Motorola's CEO, in Chicago has not only proven to be an excellent tool, leading to relevant conversations between bosses and subordinates, but has also provided a quantifiable number of positive and negative replies. It worked in the United States, where transparency and accountability have a motivating effect. However, during one of these tests in South Korea there was a sudden 98 percent "yes," and this at a site where local chip production was anything but successful. After a number of interviews with the Koreans it became very clear that they appreciated the dialoging system introduced by head office, but that only the videos and handbooks full of details had any impact on their effectiveness. Why was it only possible to answer "yes" or "no"? In Korea the answer to the boss will always be "yes," regardless of the type of question asked. And why was there this need to measure and publish those "yeses" and "nos?" The quality of the underlying philosophy was, however, highly appreciated.

An intelligent HR official in Chicago cottoned on rapidly. In parts of Asia the system has now been introduced with similar questions, but with the dichotomous yes/no replaced by a scale, so that an apparent "yes" is, at 90 percent, a subtle indicator of a Korean "no." In order to avoid loss of face the results by department are not revealed to the public.

For years Shell and Mars have used the "Basic Appraisal Quality" system of Muller and Van Lennep. The potential of employees was reviewed annually based on five criteria: analytical power, sense of reality, imagination, effective leadership and "helicopter view" (as we have already seen, the power to encompass both details and the whole). You will realize immediately that these competencies are culturally determined. Research in Europe showed that in France imagination was seen as the most important criterion; in Germany it was effective leadership; in England, power of analysis, and in the Netherlands having a good sense of reality was seen as the most important factor for rising in the local organization (there imagination had a negative correlation with potential). It will not surprise you that at Shell analytical realists – with all the helicopter view of a mole, as some cynics would say – had the best chances of climbing high.

How can we minimize the cultural factor in the assessment of people? In my last HR project for Shell we did some interesting experiments by not scoring people on these mutually exclusive competencies separately. In the year-long experiment we assessed employees on the field of tension between analytical and integral power, between a sense of reality and imagination and between rational and intuitive qualities. At each field of tension three scores were noted: two for every one of the polar qualities and one for the degree to which the candidate combined both. Thus we created three "helicopters." More recent research showed that the sum of the values of the three complementary orientations were much more strongly related to the potential of the employees than the system of five separate orientations that had been used for more than twenty years. Also, they seemed to be equally useful, whatever the culture in which they were used.

The dilemmas with which internationally operating HR professionals are confronted can thus be united on a higher level. One can attain integrity in a diversity of orientations if the HR systems contain a variety of balanced scorecards. One necessary condition, however, is that the philosophy of the policy is on such a level that a multiplicity of applications is possible in differing cultural surroundings.

CLOSING THE CULTURAL GAP BETWEEN R&D AND MARKETING

At the moment, successful organizations are linked to the way they deal with the cultural differences that surround them and the degree to which organizational culture receives the attention it deserves. Many books and articles aim at making their readers understand these differences. Much less attention is given on how to take advantage of them for organizational success.

It is remarkable just how little attention is paid to the cultural differences that can come into play within an organization. Talk at random to any employee of an innovative organization and you will receive confirmation that the relationship between Research and Development and Marketing is its Achilles heel. Our 65,000 person database also confirms that the orientation of both functional groups differ significantly. The manifestations of this tense relationship are revealed in three main areas. First of all researchers often complain that Marketing rarely allows them enough time to deliver an adequate piece of work: "Marketing gives us too little time to develop, test and fine-tune a product. This frequently leads to discrepancies between the expectations of a client and the delivered goods. In these cases most of the profits are lost in upgrading the product to the originally expected standard." In contrast, marketeers often complain about the lack of flexibility and reaction speed of R&D. Research undertaken by Trompenaars Hampden-Turner into differences of time horizons between both functional groups shows that the time horizon of the marketing function is significantly shorter than that of those working in R&D. Moreover, the R&D employee is also much more universalistic than the marketeer, in particular than the sales person. This last group seems to move from one exceptional situation to the next, which drives the researcher up the wall.

A second source of misunderstanding seems to be in the area of communication. Here also our research supports the view that R&D people often communicate in a direct, specialized, and specific tone. Their use of language is to the point but only understood by a small group because of the jargon they often use. Marketeers tend to use rather flowery language, which is less to the point. As a result, the easiest solution seems to be to stop communication all together. Obviously, this leads to significant problems, in particular to the complaint of researchers that they are too little involved in the marketing process.

Finally, the lack of understanding of each other's work and culture seems to be one of the main reasons for the tension in their relationship: "Marketing often doesn't do enough work to find out the full possibilities within a market...a large portion of their time is given to the development of a market that ultimately doesn't exist." And marketeers counter-attack: "If researchers had just a little more imagination and lived slightly less in their own world, we would have significantly fewer coordination problems." Here too a fundamental cultural difference can be seen. Marketing people are inspired by the outside world; the R&D people start from within and often lack a connection with the swiftly changing world around them.

But what needs to be done to take better advantage of these different orientations? The Marketing Science Institute (1994) has conducted interesting research on how organizations can take advantage of this fundamental field of tension:

The exploration of cross-functional development groups. These so-called "skunk" groups can achieve many successes when they integrate functions on-site and, further, when they are not too badly hindered by existing bureaucratic processes. In these groups physical, linguistic, and cultural borders are very effectively overcome. Much attention, however, needs to be given to the quality of management in these groups.

Moving people between functions. Cross-functional moves between R&D and Marketing are not easy because of the specialized nature of their activities. Starting with the recruitment phase one needs to work at attracting people who can be useful across functions and can be placed in a variety of environments. Moreover, focused internal development programs need to support the mobility of staff.

The development of informal social systems. This aim is not easily achieved because it cannot be forced upon people, but recreational activities can encourage informal social interaction in a light-hearted way. Here too, much can be achieved by minimizing the physical distance between the functions. Fruitful collaboration often occurs unexpectedly around central coffee points.

Changing the organizational design. GE and Philips have many coordination groups that bring together specializations in a balanced way. With good management stimulating cross-fertilization, many cultural and linguistic barriers can be crossed. The matrix organization is another option in which functional specialists carry on reporting to their particular boss and have a "dotted line" responsibility toward the project leader.

A more focused reward system. It appears that marketing staff very often have a variable reward system that is linked to market share. Developers frequently receive their bonus on the basis of technological developments. A reward system that is very much dependent on how much information is transferred across functions will have a very positive effect on the revenues and profitability of a company.

Formal management processes such as project management can add much to the effectiveness of the integration between R&D and marketing. This is how Mitsubishi, for example, developed the Quality Function Deployment (QFD) process whereby the client, via a program called "Qualityhouse," was given a coordinating role between marketing and R&D. Such processes seem to decrease market uncertainties as well as having a positive effect on the innovative power of an organization.

However, even in the event of an organization following all of the above advice, ultimate success will depend on the quality of leadership and the organizational culture in which these processes need to unfold.

MARKETING DILEMMAS

Marketing professionals from internationally operating organizations have long been aware of the impact of culture. They have also finally realized that this extends beyond the language used in advertising and branding. A typical example of this was when GM introduced the Chevy Nova in Mexico, not realizing that *no va* means "no go" in Spanish. Another example was when Procter & Gamble introduced the same type of Pampers in Japan as those sold in the US. Its 10 percent market share very quickly disappeared as the Japanese competition produced a much thinner version of these diapers. It turned out that Japanese mothers change their babies' diapers far more frequently than American mothers, disliking the idea of their children sitting in thick, possibly wet, diapers.

Experts have developed diverse approaches on how to respond to cultural differences. Where a product promotes local character, people tend to implement local adjustments in such areas as local distribution and advertising strategy. However, cultural differences are not always correctly taken into account.

Kodak introduced an advertisement that played on the "memory lane" theme, something that really appeals to the American psyche. In more neutral Britain the advertisement was seen as overly senti-mental. Michael Porter proclaims that Germans do not know what marketing is; in his typically American perception, marketing should – among other things – be a process whereby products are praised without inhibition. The Germans and Dutch often interpret this as boasting, something they associate with second-hand car salesmen. The way that you show the positive characteristic of a product in Europe is much more subtle, and this subtlety often escapes Porter.

When a product has a more global character, usually an American product or lifestyle, people tend to go for the universal approach. It is interesting to note that "global" also means "superficial" in German. This happens frequently with the interpretation of the uni-versal message.

Some people believe that international success depends on exploiting new global trends. Since English has become the universal language of business, developing parts of the world are no longer able to remove themselves from global markets, capital movements, and world-class standards. Procter & Gamble synchronizes many of its TV spots in local languages; what you see and what you hear is not always coordinated. Advertisements from McDonald's and Coca-Cola are not always a model of local sensitivity. "Who cares, you are buying America here," is the implicit message.

Through the advancing process of internationalization one can observe an interesting new logic developing, especially in the approach to the marketing dilemmas that arise when a global brand is experienced very differently in diverse local environments. Heineken is a good example. It is one of the best-known products in the world, but if you look at how people experience beer at the local level you will be amazed at the differences. In the 1990s Heineken embarked on the road to global marketing. The Dutch approach originally used in Holland failed miserably elsewhere. The typically Dutch meaning did not come across in a number of countries: Take, for example, an ad in which an attractive young woman is frantically looking through her closet for a nice dress. At the moment when she is most stressed her boyfriend enters. He throws her a leather jacket. In the next scene she is seen, dressed in jeans, sitting fully relaxed in a bar, drinking a Heineken. "Beer as Beer is Meant to Be" is the slogan – from stress to relaxation. This commercial failed in Greece. People interpreted it as though only failures drank Heineken. After all, how can you, as an attractive young woman, go out in your jeans if you take your partner seriously?

What can you do if you have a local product with a world reputation? Several marketing dilemmas emerge when you have to go local with a global product.

There are two possibilities of reconciling this dilemma at a higher level. At the time, Heineken again decentralized all advertising campaigns, conforming, however, to a "loose and chained" formula. They decided to centralize the European campaign. All local marketing outfits were given the freedom to develop their own campaign according to the following rules: Heineken beer had to come across as a beer of premium quality (imported) and the transition from a stressed state to a relaxed one had to be highlighted. *Beer as Beer is meant to be.* The universal joined with the local: The global message joined with the local version. This is one example of what Charles Hampden-Turner called "contextualizing" in our book *Riding the Waves of Culture;* the context is the philosophy, whereby the text refers to local habits.

In the Caribbean, Heineken tried another approach. They launched a campaign where Heineken was shown as a beer drunk by cosmopolitan people. The commercial contained shots with people in Paris, London, Tokyo, and New York, and ended with a shot of a well-known monument on one of the local islands for which it was intended. See the subtle difference? The universal product and the international lifestyle are portrayed here as universal but with local connections. Text and context interchange.

Finally, look at how McDonald's made a comeback in North America at the end of the 1990s. After a number of years of significant losses McDonald's chose a new approach. Due to the Asian crisis, its Indonesian restaurants were forced to sell rice instead of fries, which met with great success. In Europe, it introduced the McFlurry in

Vienna, different salad dressings in Paris, the McKroket in Amsterdam, and, in the Middle East, the Vegiburger. These local variations did so well that they were successfully introduced in the United States as well, resulting in improved turnover. To me, this is another success story, where the local best practices were globalized. These reconciliations are often very subtle, but their success is unparalleled.

THE CULTURAL ASPECTS OF BRANDING

The internalization of marketing poses new challenges for a lot of experts. Take one more example, a riddle that puzzled the American marketing manager of Unilever Japan. He was faced with a significant decrease in sales and market share of its Sunsilk shampoo. Traditional market research failed to show any concrete reasons for this: What do you expect, was the reaction – traditional Japanese double-talk. The drastic fall in sales followed the introduction of a new commercial in which a young woman washed her hair and dried it afterwards. Slow-motion movements contributed to the ad's sensuality, her hair making a slow, undulating swing. Then suddenly her doorbell rang and a close-up showed a man's hand opening the door. The brand then appeared on the screen.

Clotaire Rapaille describes, in 7 Secrets of Marketing in a Multicultural World, how you can decode the archetype of this product with certain "imprinting sessions." Shampoo doesn't only consist of functional characteristics, but is also a part of the surrounding culture. You need to go back to the archetype of the product, and in the US this is done by linking the product with a certain sensuality. So far, so good – but the US is not Japan. Japanese women were shown the commercial and asked to describe what they they thought the man was going to do after he opened the door. A lot of them wrote "he takes a sword and cuts her head off" – and Unilever knew why sales had gone down. The archetypes of the brand and product may be universal; the messages are culturally determined.

Although that example is about messages, the outer rim of our cultural onion, we can also see cultural misunderstandings that go to the level of basic assumptions. A number of years ago the Japanese company NTT asked the cable division of AT&T to produce a cable on the basis of a number of technical specifications. The cables were delivered but the Americans were completely surprised when the Japanese returned them almost immediately. But they had been produced exactly according to the technical standards AT&T had been given. When asked why they were returning them, NTT answered "because they are ugly." In Japan, if something is ugly it cannot be good. The Americans at AT&T have now very well understood that today a brand is not only an enumeration of functional characteristics, but also a system of meaning and more deeply held values. The understanding and use of the deepest meaning, which was once an an interesting bonus for a product, is now a primary requirement for being successful in the longer term. In their works Clotaire Rapaille and authors like Margaret Mark and Carol Pearson offer a number of interesting concepts and tools in order to map the archetype, the deepest psychological structures of a product or service.

If one examines universally held models (for example, those of Jung or Maslow), it seems that humanity faces a pair of fundamental dilemmas, regardless of cultural differences. The first consists of the dilemma between the need for safety and stability, and the desire for changes to the environment. The second dilemma concerns the tension everyone feels between finding their own way as an individuals and their desire to belong to a group. On each side of both dilemmas one finds a number of archetypes. These can be applied equally to products and services.

The archetypes for the first category – independents – are the Innocent, the Explorer, and the Sage. Everyone is, in their own way, trying to escape from the group to which they belong. Thus the *Innocent* product strives for loyalty and predictability; typical examples are Coke and McDonald's. Here you can see what happens if you deviate from an archetype, as was made clear when New Coke was introduced with a sweeter taste, to compete directly with Pepsi. Coca-Cola had to return to their roots with Classic Coke, "the real thing." The *Explorer* brand does not exist in the tranquility of a naive paradise, but is in search of a better world. Good examples are Timberland, Ralph Lauren, Jeep, and Starbucks. Finally there is the *Sage* brand which wants to help the purchaser believe that an ideal world exists as you keep learning and growing in freedom and open-mindedness. In America the bookselling chain Barns & Noble would certainly belong to this archetype, as would TV icon Oprah Winfrey.

Successful products and people also exist in an opposite set of archetypes. This trio gives the customer the impression of "belonging," and these too can be approached in several ways. Pearson and Mark distinguish the the Regular Guy/Gal, the Lover, and the Jester as different ways of belonging to a larger group. The *Regular Guy/Gal* type assumes that all people are equal and avoids any type of elitist behavior. These brands are Avis ("we try harder") rather than Hertz, Visa rather than American Express, and Volkswagen rather than BMW. *Lover* brands are often present in cosmetics, fashion and travel organizations. They refer to sex appeal and beauty and, of course, Latin brands such as Chanel, Yves St. Laurent, Gucci, and Ferrari are leading the pack. Finally we have the *Jester* type, stimulating individuals to enjoy being with each other. This archetype is embodied by brands such as Pepsi and Burger King, whose identity to a large part is developed by teasing their bigger brothers Coca-Cola and McDonald's.

In order to be internationally successful with a brand you need to incorporate contradictions between the archetypes on a higher level. A splendid example of this is how Barnes & Noble transformed itself to an international brand of great integrity. After Leonard Riggio acquired the well-known but financially unhealthy Barnes & Noble, he immediately started a successful price war. He was therefore able to buy lots of other bookshops and chains on which he continued to stick the almost monk-like logo of Barnes & Noble. After he had preserved this quite independent and individualistic image by means of exploiting the strength of its brand, he designed bookshop after bookshop with a simple living room in which there were some comfortable chairs and in which coffee was served. Thus Barnes & Noble developed into a total experience where independent "Sages" could exchange their latest brilliant ideas with similar people in a community of individualists. And Barnes & Noble has grown into the largest bookshop chain in the world.

The international success of Chanel can also be explained by a subtle integration of archetypes. Although Chanel is a classic "Lover" brand, it is known that Coco Chanel herself, although quite a sexy lady, was also fiercely independent. In her eyes women could only charm men by being independent; when asked why she refused to marry one of the richest men in Europe she answered "There are a lot of Dukes of Westminster. But there is only one Chanel." And by integrating independents and lovers she gave just the right scent to successful international marketing.

THE DEEPER MEANING OF THE BRAND

The three archetypes that reflect the need to change the world could be defined as the Hero, the Rebel, and the Magician. Typical examples of *Hero* products are Federal Express and Nike ("Just Do It"), and, as an individual, this archetype is typified by Lance Armstrong, the American cyclist and four-time winner of the Tour de France after successfully fighting cancer. The archetype of the *Rebel* has the appeal of forbidden fruit. They frequently present themselves as romantic characters, those who blow a new spirit into an organization which has suffered tyranny or oppression or which has worked too long under a dominant political party. Good examples are Richard Branson, Harley-Davidson, and Apple. The third archetype is the *Magician*, the type that wants to change the world with new technologies, the Internet, biochemistry, and genetic manipulation. Splendid examples are Sony, Ritz Carlton Hotels, and the marvelous Harry Potter-like feeling that you can cross the complete world with a little bit of plastic – MasterCard.

On the other side of the tension arc, which fulfills the need of structuring the world (or if you like, giving it safety and stability), you find the three archetypes of the Caregiver, the Creator, and the Ruler. The *Caregiver* stands for altruism and is of course very popular in the health sector and in pharmaceutical, philanthropic, and welfare institutions. Brands such as Volvo, General Electric, and BT will therefore have empathy, communication, consistency, and faith as standards in their messages. The *Creator* is rather a reflection of the artist, the innovator, and the non-conformist. Splendid brands such as Sesame Street and Swatch watches have been established as such. Finally, the *Ruler* archetype stands for the control of what exists in order to avoid chaos. The Ruler dominates the world in the desire to create wealth. American Express, Microsoft, and Procter & Gamble are good examples here.

To become internationally successful you will have to integrate archetypes on a higher level, however, by avoiding dwelling on the exaggerated stereotype. For example, General Electric recognized the inherent risk of an archetype taken too far; it changed into the "Hero", improving the world by innovation (and technology). Hence, GE's well-known slogan of the 1980s – "living better electronically" – was changed to "GE – we bring good things to life." Text and context are thereby exchangeable. In Europe the accent is now being put on taking care of humanity. On television I saw a commercial in which an Italian football player had injured himself; Italian football fans cried and shouted in a typically Latin way. The player was immediately driven from the field to a GE MRI scan and, thanks to high-tech photography, was revealed as not having a serious injury. In the next frame he scored the winning goal for Italy, and there was uproar. Subsequently a GE operative was thanked by phone in an equally emotional manner, and the ad finished with the line "I am just doing my job."

The reconciliation of opposite systems of meaning, or archetypes of brands, are often significant factors in their success, making them less sensitive to cultural interpretations. By doing this, an integrated brand is created, one that doesn't go over the top in terms of mastering or changing the environment, or of being part of a community or striving for individual independence. The release of this tension is often showed through humor, as is shown in an asprin ad, turning a

"Caregiver" into a "Hero" archetype: A young couple is woken by an alarm clock at 6.30 a.m. The young man jumps out of bed and drops a tablet into a glass of water. He walks to his partner and wakes her by upending the glass over her head. She demands to know what on earth it is and he replies by saying that it's an aspirin. Baffled, she informs him that she doesn't have a headache, upon which he goes back under the sheets…The ad is brilliantly finished by "ASPRO – for worse times." The Caregiver can become a Hero in any culture. Do you agree?

THE BAKER, KPN, AND THE CUSTOMER WHO IS ALWAYS RIGHT

Being a fanatic user of the Internet I wanted to be one of the first to try the fast ASDL line. No problem. I went to the KPN.nl site and soon grasped the exciting possibilities. Included was an online service informing future users of whether it was possible to link up in their neighborhoods and, lo and behold, it was possible in mine. The site also explained that there were two authorities that needed to be approached, namely KPN for MXStream and a provider. To each their own expertise.

However, there was a difficulty. They said: "Unfortunately, there is a problem with one of your two analog lines that cannot be not dealt with at the same time as we put in the new line. We'll will make a separate appointment, disconnect putting in the new line and repairing the old line." Got it? I didn't – but what choice did I have?

We managed to have the new line installed. "On Friday 14?" That suited us just fine. And on Friday 14 the line would have been installed, if it had not so happened that two months earlier a digital cable had been put in which, by chance, happened to cross the analog cable network right in front of our door. "No problem, sir," said the installers. "We'll make another appointment with another department of our company. We'll solve it, but we aren't allowed to do this ourselves." Why not? Each to their own expertise.

Ten days later more installers arrived; as before, they were most agreeable. They would put in a line underneath the digital cable hole and it would only take a minute. True, that same day I had a functioning analog line going to my home.

My wife then asked them if we could have three connections (we wanted to have a small network between our three PCs at home). "Yes, madam, that can be done, but you will have to make an appointment with our technicians; we cannot do it. If you asked them, they'd install a hub." "Can't you do that?" "Yes, but we aren't allowed to. It's another department." And they went on their way after leaving a number. Ah well, each department to its own.

Now we had a new analog line, although one of the two old ones still wasn't working. We called the service department, which – after waiting for half an hour – was able to determine that it couldn't be checked because the line had been disconnected: The bill hadn't been paid. So we called the finance department. Within 20 minutes that was fixed. I asked if this could really have been the cause of the original problem. "I don't think so," was the reply, "because you have only been disconnected for three days and the fault existed before that time, didn't it? Do you have the number of the service department? I can easily put you through, if you like."

Twenty minutes later I was advised to visit a phone shop and buy a home exchange. Off to the shop I went and after paying for my exchange I was advised to make an appointment with the technicians who would be able install the new device – for another payment. At home my wife approached me with a big smile on her face. Both lines were working again. "Probably because you paid," she said. Ho ho.

We now had a functioning home exchange and an analog line, but we were still in need of a provider. Seven months had passed and I had vanished from the provider's database. So I made another appointment. On the application form I had to fill in what speed I wanted and, if I wanted the 512/128 (the fastest, which would have been great), then the provider would have to order a new telephone line. Since I had just got one, I made a phone call. "You want the 512/128? We have to order that telephone line anyway," I was told. "No," I said, "I have already got one, based on your earlier advice." "Well," was the reply, "we will try, sir, but I don't think that you will have much luck with that service. Why don't you take the 512/64, it's the same price, but a bit slower?" "OK, I'll take that one. Just as long as we do not have to ask for any more lines to be put in," I replied angrily. "And, by the way," my adviser added, "we're not able to place a hub. You could try KPN."

It was time for professional assistance.

I contacted an IT company that would deal with all of this rubbish. They would also call KPN and the provider. It was wonderful: "If you just go on holiday, we'll make sure that everything works within three weeks," I was told.

At least I learned one thing. I know people at the mill that break up the grain; I can get yeast, milk from the cow, and salt from the mine. But I still go to the baker. He will take care of all of that for me. The finished product is called bread. My baker has a flourishing bakery, because he knows what I want.

There is still hope for KPN. Everyone to whom I spoke on the telephone was very friendly, understood my frustration and all came to the same conclusion: "We could help you, but we are not allowed to." That is the sign of a flawed organization. More can be done to solve this than just hiring experts to fill in the gaps. Paying more attention to stakeholders than to shareholders would constitute a good start.

FIVE DILEMMAS OF KNOWLEDGE MANAGEMENT

Once upon a time Peter and Gordon sang "To know, know, know you is to love, love, love you." In the last decade knowledge management has gained an important place in management thinking and it is a crucial process within the learning organization. The development from an industrial to a knowledge economy has been the major reason for its popularity but, as with the latest managements fads around MBO (management by objectives) and teamwork, it is also a response to the omission of certain values in Western society.

To process knowledge effectively has perhaps become today's most important competitive advantage. It determines the innovative competence, the way you can apply and retain the core competencies within an organization, and the way the organization learns. Effective knowledge management is dependent on the type of organizational culture in which it reconciles dilemmas. We have identified five:

The Universal versus the Particular. A process controller with Motorola once told me that some time ago he had been trying to improve the cleaning process of electronic circuits on GSMs. By using sharper brushes he did not only clean more effectively, but also cut through many of the essential circuits. More than US$100,000 worth of damage was done.

Bob Galvin, then the CEO of Motorola, asked him to come to his room. He didn't fire the employee, but instead asked him to write a report on how these types of errors could be avoided in the future. After reading the report Galvin thanked him, because he had saved the organization more than a million dollars. Knowledge management is only effective when you create an error-correcting system that learns continuously from one-off mistakes. In the long run, there is nothing more dangerous than an errorless system.

Individual versus Team knowledge. Perhaps it is individualizing Western society that provides the ultimate drive for our need for knowledge management. Educational systems are based on accumulating knowledge individually. Students are entered into a competitive game in which only the fittest survive; however, the organizations in which the graduates come to work pay a price. Communitarian cultures such as France and Japan face the opposite problem. A Canadian student once appealed forcefully to my intercultural knowledge and experience. In his university in Montreal the French students were not operating on a level playing field with their American colleagues. Almost all French students cheated during their exams by sharing information with each other. How could you ever respect this even by understanding cultural differences in a non-judgmental way? "Knowledge management," I whispered in his ear. French people, like the Japanese, have a much greater talent for joint preparation and the sharing of knowledge among colleagues.

Americans have an opposite challenge: How to share individually gained knowledge with a group. During my stay at Wharton a fellow student had solved this challenge creatively. All the chapters that we needed to read for the next exam were removed from the relevant books. Nobody else could get to that material. Well, knowledge remains a relative concept, if one student is set up against the others for competitive grading.

Specific and Codified versus Diffuse and Implicit Knowledge. Many organizations have a treasure trove of implicit or "tacit" knowledge, in the words of Nonaka and Takeuchi; their success will depend on how this can be transferred into something concrete, an explicit product. In their book *The Knowledge-creating Company* they use Matsushita's development of the world's first fully automated home bakery machine as an example. When the inventors couldn't fully understand the mechanism for kneading the dough, one of their software programmers was apprenticed to the top baker at the Osaka International Hotel. Only after he had mastered the implicit knowledge of dough kneading was he able to transfer this information to his engineer colleagues.

Americans have a mirror image of this experience. When guiding the integration of the Japanese Isuzu Trucks with General Motors' Truck Division, we noticed that the Americans were quite upset by the Japanese. The Americans used about 30 percent of their time to codify and write up their knowledge in handbooks and procedures. However, the knowledge of the Japanese was stored in their network of relationships. Do you need any written documents in order for the members of your family to understand each other? The Americans reacted to this situation by asking how one could ever learn and transfer that knowledge and experience, if it wasn't written up. We suggested explaining to the Japanese how to write effective handbooks; much shorter and efficient manuals of explicit knowledge were the result. The Americans had chosen a type of reasoning in which the interaction with the Japanese created a bond that enabled knowledge to be stored on the network.

Top Down versus Bottom Up. Data about clients and products are stored in the heads of individual staff members. Middle management translates this into information that in turn is organized as knowledge by top management. For effective knowledge management the reconciliation of this dilemma can be found in "middle–up–down," in which middle management is the bridge between the standards of top management and the chaotic reality of those in the front line. In addition the knowledge of top management is often just as crucial in organizing and defining the information coming from within the organization.

From Inside Out to Outside In. Effective knowledge management is not constrained by the walls of the organization. Inner-oriented cultures prefer to start from enhancing the internal processes; externally oriented cultures prefer to start with the insights and needs of the client. The internal and external environments need to be amalgamated in order to attain not a "balanced," but an "integrated" scorecard, in which the client has a direct influence on internal processes. This, in turn, serves to increase the client's own knowledge.

In all these dilemmas the context of organizational culture dictates the preference for a specific starting point for reconciliation, but effective knowledge management is dictated by the integrated scorecard of rules and exceptions, groups and individuals, explicit and implicit, top and bottom, and, finally, inner and outer worlds.

CHAPTER 6

Globalization

In the process of globalization, a number of key dilemmas are observed to arise again and again, across the world.

GLOBAL AND LOCAL IN JAPAN

People often ask me whether globalization will cause cultures to resemble each other more and more, but the question is difficult to answer. For example, even after a recent major assignment in Japan it remains hard to say whether that country is becoming "global" or will remain "local."

For the Japanese, the only way to survive seems to be to internationalize their businesses away from their high-contextual local environment. Until now Japanese organizations have frequently created dual hierarchies and organizations when they go abroad. But this splitting of a local touch and Tokyo-led management abroad has led to many overlapping responsibilities and inefficiency. The absence of reconciliation between Japanese and local management has resulted in serious financial consequences for those international organizations with their origins in Japan. Thus there is a need to consider how integration with non-Japanese management can be established, given that the results from successful integration can be mind-blowing.

The team my colleague Peter Prud'homme and I worked with on

our recent assignment was very international. It was led by a French CEO, who had an American MBA, and consisted of fifteen Japanese, a number of Englishmen, a Swede, and an Australian.

Explaining cultural differences was easy as the organization itself was sufficiently international. However, our assignment was to build a multicultural team combining the best of all cultures. At the kick-off meeting we were pretty certain that the most important conditions for success were already present. Firstly, a charismatic Frenchman was at the helm with clear objectives based on a clear vision; building a successful team starts with the quality of the leadership and a desire to work toward shared objectives. There was also a willingness and desire to learn from and listen to each other.

The French CEO kicked off with a well-known joke.

An American was to go to Japan and talked to a colleague who had a wealth of Japan-based experience beforehand. This person advised him never to open with a funny story, but to start by being completely serious. The American objected; making things less serious was his strength. So he began his speech in Japan with a good joke. After the translation all the Japanese burst out laughing. "You see," the American said, "my jokes are beyond culture." "No," replied his colleague, "The Japanese translator explained that this was a typical American joke and asked the audience to laugh so you didn't lose face."

The scene had been set. The group laughed, and spontaneously this time, too.

Despite this the workshop did not start smoothly. We asked the participants to give a definition of culture. The English quickly came up with "The way we do things around here." The Frenchman mentioned "raison d'être." Interestingly the Swede came up with a description that had "harmony" at its core. Even when defining culture it is difficult to circumvent cultural backgrounds. After the break we introduced a traditional West–East distinction. The Protestant urge for universal values (standardization, globalization, abstraction, contracts) contrasted sharply with the Japanese love for particularism (flexibility, localization, concreteness, and relationships).

The Japanese only really took off after we asked the participants to share their personal experiences in small groups. They described those from the West by using words such as "kyakkanteki" and "shukanteki", Japanese for objectivity and subjectivity, meaning respectively the guests' and the hosts' point of view. The Japanese do not have other words for these concepts. Where someone from the West tries to build a relationship unrelated to the subject, the Japanese feels a need to start a process of bringing different viewpoints together. The first discussion concluded that more should be done to use Japanese viewpoints and local views as the input for developing standards in Great Britain and Sweden.

Communication styles form a big problem between Japanese and, in particular, Swedes and Australians. Many times these specific Westerners tend to dominate meetings, because of their being to the point and presenting clear summaries. Foreigners often see the contextual approach of the Japanese as being indirect, diffuse, and unclear. Quite apart from that, the Japanese may often be reluctant to give their opinions in a meeting where some loss of face could be experienced. The solution the participants came up with was as simple as it was brilliant. Meetings should be shorter and the extra time should be filled with small informal meetings with more room for use of the Japanese language, and where the fear of possible loss of face would be reduced because of the intimacy of the gathering. It started working on the spot. I have rarely seen Japanese people make such concrete and funny presentations. This was only possible because, during preparation, they had been able to work on the context.

Although Japan Inc. has major problems in globalizing – because of its closed culture where "nemawashi" (networking) is essential for effectiveness – it is clear that the integration of local and global is possible. Making Japanese and Westerners work together effectively does, however, require competent leadership able to reconcile cultural dilemmas. The leader also needs to facilitate communication between cultures around clear objectives, which cannot be open to questioning.

We would like to suggest this approach to Western companies in Japan – work on effective teams which, through well-selected foreign leadership, can create great synergies. This could also help Japanese organizations to be more active in Europe and America. They are often very ineffective because these conditions have not been fulfilled. On many occasions the result of that is a dual organization of artless Japanese and frustrated local managers.

I sometimes compare Japan with a fugu, a fish with poisonous glands. If you prepare it well, it's a highly appreciated delicacy; without this expertise, eating it may lead to serious food poisoning. In the majority of cases well-educated foreign "cooks" surpassed the quality of their Japanese equivalents; Japan can only become international with the help of foreigners. So there is hope still. Such cooks will make it possible for Japan to internationalize effectively.

WHY THE MATRIX FAILS IN FRANCE

It is good to see that in the world of management, history also repeats itself. When I studied business economy in the mid 1970s, a lot of attention was given to the matrix structure of organizations. Now, much later, it seems that increasing globalization has brought this despised but popular way of organizing back into focus. The increasing complexity and variation of the environment and the organization itself have contributed to this. When one takes into consideration the decrease of the number of management layers, the rebirth of the matrix is easy to explain.

In the past decade we have fully concentrated our attention on core activities and "profit centers," forgetting the importance of the dual hierarchy. Those organizations that have turned dual authority into second nature are now often rudely awakened – because it is being covered by a third, often regional, dimension.

But, just as before, cultural aspects are still excessively neglected during restructuring. Even at the end of the 1970s, André Laurent, the French INSEAD professor, wrote an article entitled "Why the Matrix Organization Failed in France." I often added the subtitle "What didn't?" because I hadn't seen much working properly there.

However, it is not only in this beautiful country that typically Anglo-Saxon structures and processes are failing. We see, again, that many American and English companies continue to divide their organizations into incompatible compartments. With their Anglo-Saxon task-oriented and project approach that does not seem to present any problems. Authority is depersonalized and the power of the outcome of the project or task is considered to be beyond personal objectives or political games.

Within this system consensus is reached between conflicting organizational coalitions within a reasonable amount of time. One of the basic laws of this textbook matrix is that problems are to be solved at the level on which they appear. You are only allowed to involve a higher level of management in case of emergency; otherwise management would very quickly become overwhelmed. Besides this, matrix structure – and project structure in particular – assumes a limit to the way managers think. Projects have to be finished on time and accomplish agreed-upon objectives. The organization is simply an instrument, nothing more. The responsible person's power is based upon their knowledge and expertise, and that's the end of it. That is also why managers are supposed to change positions often; mobility is a prerequisite.

I have already made several implicit cultural assumptions above, and that also pinpoints the problems of international implementation of the matrix structure. For example, French culture, as part of the greater Latin culture, does not live up to these prerequisites. Power is individual power; it belongs to someone personally, not by virtue of their task or role. In this family culture we often observe that a conflict between managers is also a test of subordinates' loyalty, assuming that they will always support their line manager. The logic of the task is way too abstract in a French organization that is dependent on personal trust. This constitutes the death of the dualistic hierarchy. Time limits, prevalent in a project-by-project approach, are anathema in France, where one's history is equally as important as one's future. You only have to look at the delightful distinction in French grammar between the *imparfait* and *passé composé*, and try to explain that to English-speaking people.

But why do Germans seem to have so many problems with the matrix? After all, power is depersonalized and German projects are, of course, always finished on time. The crazy thing is that German organizational culture often ascribes power to the role/function instead of to the task. Then the genie escapes from the matrix "bottle." There will often be a conflict between the function and the expertise that should come with it. In this situation Germans often dig their heels into the ground whereas Americans tend to choose to finish the project. For them the task has priority, even though this may damage their position.

From the above it appears that the matrix organization is actually the organizational symbol of a dilemma: the dilemma of hierarchy versus conflicting logics. It is also an intercultural dilemma. Dual and tertiary matrices are more often regular occurrences than exceptions. Does this mean that we should simply install Americans in crucial spots where they can happily practice their cultural deficiencies? I see enough examples of this among American companies. What a waste of talent!

Strangely enough the metaphor of the family, the most simplistic of matrices, may give us a solution. The family also has a dual hierarchy and children will often (ab)use this. And yet, the effective parent, like no other (once again I hear my wife laughing out loud), knows how to play along with the other parent when children are around, in order to establish their personal position of power. This will often happen in order to complete the tasks the family or the parents have set themselves. To accomplish this the "managers" will have to communicate frequently, often without the daily pressure of ongoing projects. Dilemmas also have to be made transparent and discussed. At that time you often see that the parents' different personalities become complementary rather than mutually destructive, and so it is in the world of matrices between cultures.

Excellent organizations like Unilever, GE, and Shell have definitively shown that, used in this way, matrix thinking becomes an art rather than a structure. And that will even work with the French.

REMOTE MANAGEMENT IS A MATTER OF TRUST

Managing people from a distance isn't new. The Roman Empire showed striking examples of what is popularly known as remote management. Then, as now, success was determined by the extent to which the players met a number of requirements.

In the last ten years there has been an increasing need to manage remotely. In the first phase of the process of internationalization, when only the export of products and services had to be facilitated, it was relatively simple. Within the multi-local organization we often see (expatriate) managers living close to their "troops." With the birth of the transnational organization we can see that managers have to be active in many regions at the same time and that physical presence becomes increasingly problematic. On top of that markets have become fragmented and, therefore, must be managed by local staff. Finally, the number of layers within organizations has been reduced considerably and the opportunities for communicating with each other via email, the Internet, videoconferences, and mobile telecommunications have significantly improved.

I have noticed the composition of remote teams becoming international more often, and the management of such teams will be even more complex. A manager of remote teams must at least have the same competencies as a regular manager working with cross-cultural teams. That is already tough enough. However, little attention is given in today's literature to additional competencies that are needed.

A successful manager of international remote teams will go through the same (six) phases as when the teams are located in the same building, whereby certain aspects ask for more or less attention. First, the manager should always be physically present when selecting teams. However, this selection should be enriched by extra criteria. It appears that a person's communication style, learning style, and family circumstances are crucial to operating effectively in a virtual team. There are sound instruments available to provide insights into this matter.

After selection, in the second phase, it is time to build relationships. The team's core players need a chance to build trust in each other's presence by discussing the team's objectives and the processes and style they want apply in order to achieve those objectives. The manager could facilitate the discussion of the various communication styles and concurrent dilemmas may emerge.

The third phase contains the articulation of the objectives and roles of different team players. To facilitate this process there are various instruments available. As previously mentioned, I personally find the work of Meredith Belbin very useful in determining various roles within a team and in enabling the team to use the complementary characteristics of its members to achieve the planned goals.

Unexpected misinterpretations of roles can be fatal. Take one example: During remote surgery a surgeon, located in Brussels, asked the nurse, located in Düsseldorf, to turn the scalpel 20 degrees. To dismay of the Belgian surgeon she refused, using the words "In Germany a nurse does not have permission to do that." The surgery failed.

In this phase the members of a team should spend time in each other's presence. Only from the fourth and fifth phases are individual and team performance addressed. Team members then agree on how they determine what works and what does not work on both levels. It is important for the remote manager to make clear which criteria will be used to judge the performance of the team and the individual, including the way in which this is monitored and the team members are given feedback.

Finally, the sixth phase focuses on the process of learning and (continuous) improvement. In order to do this properly the team should meet regularly.

In 1985, when Boris Becker was the youngest player ever to win Wimbledon, tennis became extremely popular in Germany. In order to meet the demand for tennis lessons, skiing coaches started to teach tennis. It is true that skiing coaches do not know much about playing tennis, but they did know a good deal about sports and about how to move. The result was that at the end of the tennis season those students who had received lessons from skiing coaches could play much better than the students who had had their lessons with tennis coaches. The skiing coaches' students were given much more leeway to correct their own mistakes. As a consequence, their learning curve was much steeper.

These are the basic conditions for reconciling core dilemmas when managing remotely. The first dilemma has everything to do with communication. How can people from a high-context culture – where intonation, non-verbal communication, and the holistic perspective determine the meaning of a particular message – communicate with people from a low-context culture who explicitly say what something is about? The scarce literature on remote management pays much attention to the benefits of using the right communication channels, like the Internet, email, voicemail, and videoconferencing. However, these don't solve the problem, because they are all means of communication that are fairly low context.

Two processes can make communications more effective by increasing the context. Besides low context methods like email, it is recommended that people subsequently call and expand the available resources, the scale or the context. This is not about the separate means that are at your disposal, but about combining them. A brief phone call after sending an email to your Japanese colleague may work wonders. If team members further agree to meet once a week on a special website or by telephone conference (taking time differences into consideration) to discuss mutual challenges, it can be made to work very well, especially if the manager is in attendance.

Finally, team members need to meet face-to-face on a regular basis. Attendance of the entire team at such meetings is a prerequisite. Obviously, meetings need to be organized in such a way that many business issues can be discussed effectively, leaving sufficient time available for informal contact. In this way remote meetings encompass the proper context.

Actually, the same applies in a family. The more children trust their parents, the easier it is for them to stay with friends. Trust only grows when the family convenes at the right moments around collective challenges.

RISK MANAGEMENT ACROSS CULTURES

Recently, Risk Management has been the subject of much attention, and rightly so. Political and economic situations worldwide seem more turbulent than ever. Do different cultures really cope with these changes in different ways? And are there cultures that take risks more easily than others?

Were you to read Hofstede you would think that there were significant differences between the desire of cultures to reduce uncertainty. This conclusion is drawn a bit too quickly. If you dig a little deeper then you will see that his questionnaire only looked at how the Dutch would avoid uncertainty using questions such as: "How many years do you foresee yourself working with your organization?" "Do you often feel stressed at work?" and "Rules set by an organization should not be broken, not even if it would be in the best interest of the organization. Do you agree?" Well, it may be that there are differences in the degree to which they avoid uncertainty. However, a much more important factor relates to the different ways in which people try to reduce uncertainty and the motivation underlying those uncertainties they want to reduce. For example, every culture knows the dilemma between caution and courage. If you are only cautious you are likely to encounter almost as many risks as the reckless. When I prune our trees from a ladder, my wife warns me to be careful. If, however, I were to renege on this task because of my slight fear of heights, she would say that I ought to show some courage. We all want to avoid uncertainty – be it the possibility of falling or being seen as weak by others – but we have our own ways of doing so.

One example of a culturally determined strategy for addressing risk goes as follows. I came across a Chinese executive who said that he felt insecure about a business transaction because his American counterpart was so persistent on getting the contract signed: "I do not trust him, because how can I trust someone who wants so desperately to have a contract signed?" The American said the contrary: "I only trust the Chinese now that he has signed the contract." Between cultures one can best reduce these uncertainties by celebrating the universal symbol of the contract after having established the particular relationship.

A second cultural determinant of accepting risks is expressed in the degree to which the responsibility of the risks is assumed to be taken by the individual or the group. An Asian will experience contributing to a pension at the age of thirty in a different way from an individualistic American or a Dutch person. In a communitarian culture the risks associated with growing old are still taken care of by the family, while people in western cultures cling more to the safety net of pension funds and social welfare programs for the elderly.

Also, at the level of business you can see that the corporate culture has a certain effect on risk avoidance. In a recent study by PricewaterhouseCoopers it appears that Western banks still split their risks into different, deceptively neat, areas – credit, market, and operational risks – rather than accepting that these risks could be intertwined. More specific cultures generally have the tendency to segment risks into areas such as financial and non-financial or qualitative and quantitative. In comparison, in more holistic and diffuse cultures such as Japan, people see that in management all risks are linked. Both world views, at their extreme, have a sub-optimal result. To revisit an example I looked at earlier – in the Netherlands, banks will be at your service right up until the moment you are at risk and really need help. The Japanese banks accept so much risk that if things go wrong the bank itself will be heavily involved in the financial mess. Here you can also see that risks can best be managed if the leaders of the organizations concerned take a holistic view of divided risks. It is for very good reasons that the fastest growing role in American business is that of the Chief Risk Officer. Moreover, according to a study by KPMG, this integration of risks is often missing, and could be well taken care of within Enterprise Risk Management. Besides this, long-term-oriented cultures often choose investments in well-established companies with high status and a proven track record. Short-term-oriented cultures are more inclined to invest in upcoming businesses, for example in the high-tech sector. Ultimately one can see that, internationally, you are best equipped with a well-informed portfolio manager who invests in funds where both kinds of investments are being reconciled.

A final culturally determined strategy to reduce risk is dependent on the way in which a group of people relates to their environment. Cultures that believe they can control their external environment will use all means to block out any possible risk by increasing their measures of control. *Business Week* recently ran an article entitled

"Firepower for Financial Cops," suggesting that if we were to re-invent the Securities Exchange Commission we would need to hire more cops who would be authorized to break up overly concentrated accounting firms, to tap telephones, and to launch criminal cases against wrongdoers. Cultures that feel the environment is controlling them have a different way of limiting risk. A good example is Shell's investment in the development of pig farms in the Philippines in order to support the local population and thus reduce rebel sabotage of pipelines. A great success – you really can listen to what is happening in the community to reduce the risk of sabotage, rather than throwing more cops at people to avoid it.

Every culture will try to manage risks and avoid uncertainties. To effectively handle this in an international context, people need to see beyond their own cultural way of doing things. People need to show courage if they want to be careful. Confucius says: "To know what is right and not to do it is the worst cowardice." And Plato has stated that courage is knowing what to fear.

JUST IN TIME

Are deadlines experienced similarly around the globe? I cannot imagine that in Northern Europe and Southern Italy the same seriousness can be found around fixing precise dates and agreements. I even wonder if the Italian dictionary provides us with a good translation of the word "deadline" – *linea del morte* doesn't really sound right. Why is it that we so often explain cultural differences according to the (in)flexibility with which one deals with time?

In order to illustrate stereotypes I often quote the French who compare the Swiss to robots, planning all their activities by the clock.

They eat because it is 6.00 p.m., not because they are hungry. And if I characterize the French as people who are always late, you hear other people say: "Oh, did you hear what he said about the French?" These individuals are the worst. They do not understand that in most countries of the world it is normal to be late. It is only the North-Western Europeans and North Americans who characterize people with a flexible time orientation as "primitive." A Frenchman once explained to me very clearly that the problem of being late was only a problem for people who were punctual. People who are always on time often don't know what to do when the person they are meeting arrives late. This type of person always loses time. And the French never do; they always have something else to get on with. You can never tell exactly when someone will arrive.

Edward Hall described the way the Swiss organize time as "monochrone," while the French are "polychrone." Monochronic cultures organize time on a thin line and can only do one thing at a time. You can recognize people from these cultures when they are on the phone because they will make gestures that you should not interrupt them. You can only do one thing in a focused way. Now look at Italy – you see Italians on the phone, having a second conversation, zipping a cup of coffee, organizing themselves, and all in parallel. The polychronic Italians are used to organizing time in a band consisting of parallel lines. That is why someone who has an appointment can arrive thirty minutes late without offering any excuse; the other party will always have something else to do. In Arabic cultures it is important to pick the right day. Another way to recognize the difference is to look at the various eating and cooking habits. Monochronic cultures often have food that needs to be planned precisely; polychronic cultures love stews or beans (the longer they simmer the better they taste), or use almost-instant food like spaghetti.

It is nice to know that cultures organize time differently, but it can be problematic. How do you deal with missing figures from your Italian office that you need desperately before the end of the year? An incident that happened to my wife can provide great insights. She worked for years in the Amsterdam office of GFT who organize the Dutch distribution and administration of brands like Armani, Ungaro, and Valentino. The manager was desperate about what to do with the unpredictable Italians and their delivery times. Dutch fashion outlets count on having the summer collection in their shops by January 15, while the winter collection should be on the racks at the end of August. However, some pieces were delivered (and therefore refused) on March 1 or on October 1. At first there were reactions of denial in response to the eruptions of anger from the Dutch CEO. Thereafter, an Italian cynicism dominated: "In view of your Dutch sense of fashion you can sell the collection next year as well." When the Dutch started ordering two weeks in advance the Italians became suspicious, which resulted in an even more unpredictable delivery pattern. Fines for late delivery were paid without complaints. Italians cannot be influenced by material things like money when their pride is at stake.

As someone who was desperate the Dutch boss had overlooked the most simple of solutions. Monochrone cultures believe that the sequential order of time is dictated by a universal principle – the clock. Polychrone Italians have a particularistic feeling for time. If you care about your partner you'll make sure that you deliver on time; you don't want to cause any difficulties for people you respect. A subordinate is always on time, the boss may be late. Italians like to deliver for *you*, not for some vulgar, abstract clock. We advised the Dutch boss to take three weeks vacation in Italy and use the opportunity to organize some dinners with his Italian counterparts. We also advised him not to forget to include invitations to the heads of logistics. From then on he never had any problems with late deliveries – though later we did hear that the Swedish agents were running into trouble.

NEW DILEMMAS FOR SHELL

My partner Charles Hampden-Turner and I have accumulated some twenty-five years of experience with the Shell organization. It all started in the 1980s. Charles was a consultant at the impressive Group Planning and I was a freshly graduated economist. When we were interviewing Shell's president Sir Mark Moody-Stuart recently, we asked ourselves how Shell was approaching more recent dilemmas. It was striking how introverted Shell had become during the last decades; it seemed that the quality of its internal communication was in reverse proportion to what it was doing externally.

Internally, everyone agreed that Shell was a cosmopolitan company with high integrity. For example, Shell provided the opportunity for each of its employees make an annual donation to a non-profit organization. When this applied to me, I decided that my own donation would go to a kindergarten where two my our children were given guidance during the day. After a week of deep thought and consideration its management decided it could not accept "blood money" from Shell. At that time South Africa was focus of daily discussion and, according to outsiders, Shell was playing a dubious role. As a Shell employee I was irritated by the fact that very interesting and positive facts known to the insiders were not communicated openly with the outside world.

Moody-Stuart, who joined Shell's Committee of Managing Directors in 1991, claims that Shell's external communication has been drastically changed after the serious problems caused by the misunderstandings around its North Sea platform Brent Spar and its activities in Nigeria. According to him Shell had high integrity, but it was Shell's own integrity based on its own rationalities and judgments. Just consider Brent Spar. Everything was well calculated. But public opinion turned against Shell because it was maneuvred into an incorrect position. Greenpeace announced – with much media attention – that the platform contained 4,000 tons of oil deposits. This information was not correct, but by the time Greenpeace apologized for their mistake it didn't matter any more. In Nigeria Shell was confronted with something similar. Shell thought it had right on its side, but failed to communicate its argument effectively.

The prevailing logic looks much more like that of the Swedish minister for environmental affairs. She also thought that Shell's arguments were completely correct, but had a problem. How could we explain to our children that recycling was good if one of the largest corporations in the world just dumped its rubbish on the bottom of the ocean? One is concerned here with a non-technical logic but one that is full of emotions, conviction, and symbolic gestures. What Shell is trying to do, according to Moody-Stuart, is to reconcile the two logics. After the execution of the Nigerian activist Ken Saro-Wiwa Shell had very convincing factual materials at its disposal, and was fully convinced about the fact that it took the right steps at the time.

The underlying dilemma is concerned with the truth and whether it is fully transferable to others. According to Moody-Stuart, in the future Shell will need to discuss matters even more openly with the relevant parties. In discussions with the media, politicians, and the public Shell's dilemmas need to be transformed into mutual dilemmas, shared by the community, because that is what they are a part of. This assumes, however, that Shell's internally directed culture will change.

A second dilemma that Shell has recently approached is their version of global/local. Shell's organization has become known as a decentralized multi-local one, held together by strongly centralized financial and HR systems and some 8,000 expatriates. The latter move from country to country to exchange the best practices and to gain consensus for most of the decisions they take. Toward the end of the twentieth century it looked as though the speed and radius of the decisions needed to increase; Shell seemed to be less effective than Exxon and BP.

In 1997 we saw the beginning of drastic changes in Shell when the US company Shell Oil was fully integrated and North Americans started to occupy key positions which had previously been filled by the British and the Dutch. In addition, the power of the country organizations, which often grew into real kingdoms, diminished. Now decision making power is in the hands of those persons who have both functional as well as regional responsibilities. Because of the abundance of local experience of Shell employees, the organization is able to react locally and from a much broader and more global perspective.

A third area in which Shell has experienced great changes in the last decade is the process of "Trust me, I am not that stupid," ending in

"Show me that you do what you tell me that you do, so I can trust you." In the first approach the hierarchy had to be trusted unconditionally; in the second, they had to achieve and perform in order to gain people's trust. Much more questioning of authority resulted from this shift.

A fourth dilemma has developed as a result of the competition with the shareholder-focused Exxon and the more stakeholder- and communication-oriented BP. By making use of the metaphor of a three-legged chair Shell tries to show that there is no alternative to the integration of all stakeholders – and to making a contribution to the planet's supply of energy with this balance.

The fifth dilemma lies at the centre of Moody-Stuart's attention: the meritocracy. In the 1970s and 1980s the most important competence of each employee was to inflate their Currently Estimated Potential (CEP). These heavy words referred to the potential that was ascribed to them annually for the ultimate position they would occupy when they were around fifty years of age. If their potential was high enough anything they said was taken as being, at the very least, brilliant. As such the potential of people became a self-fulfilling prophecy. This assessment system worked quite well in a relatively stable environment within a long-term perspective. Today, however, one needs shorter feedback loops. And in a multicultural environment, argues Moody-Stuart, the British and Dutch cannot solely be the ones to define core competencies. Shell is searching for what different cultures value most. This could be imagination for the French, a sense of reality for the Dutch, and wisdom for the Japanese. A genuine meritocracy takes these differences into consideration. There are more definitions to which top leaders are held accountable, in particular to the way they integrate these qualities.

Shell's success in the future will be less dependent on the price of oil. In order to reconcile the dilemmas described above, Shell needs to take the best from the labor market. Shell will only be able to do so if the organization can transform itself into a player in the new economy by taking responsibility for the creation of alternative sources of energy and alternative approaches to management. Then it will not only be good for people inside Shell, but also for those far beyond its borders.

CHAPTER 7

Diversity

The topic of diversity has become increasingly important; it has become apparent that we need a "diverse approach" to diversity across the globe. But the issues are the same.

There are, obviously, different types of diversity around the world. Reconciliation is the first step to overcoming the problems caused by this. National differences are possibly more to the fore in Europe, while in the United States ethnic differences and gender are more prominent. But reconciliation is a unifying methodological framework that can help all these scenarios. Secondly, were we to have more means of measuring and quantifying such differences through databases and assessment tools, we might have more insights or a strategy for how to approach diversity issues. Most managers do not buy into the soft stuff, but once quantified and measured they feel more relaxed with it. Thirdly, I have accumulated evidence to support the proposition that it is important to have more nationalities in those groups approaching diversity; and finally, diversity programs need to be linked to business issues such as being fully integrated into a leadership program, or similar.

THE DIVERSITY OF DIVERSITY

More and more frequently clients ask Trompenaars Hampden-Turner to help them with their diversity programs. With European organizations this generally means extending existing programs on (national) cultural diversity with programs on gender and minorities. With our North American clients in Europe we often find that this request is based on fear; European HR managers from US firms are very anxious that North American methods of coping with "diversity" should be launched in Europe. There is a big chance that the results will be counter-productive.

Europeans have as much need for the integration of minorities as Americans, but it is the predominance of quantitative American measures that frightens them, and for good reasons. In the United States laws have already been applied making it easier for minorities to enter US corporations, based on statistics. On top of that, many workshops are being organized to make the Caucasian male aware of his (often unconscious) politically incorrect behavior. In the US there is also quite a lot of discussion as to the effectiveness of these types of approaches, and Europeans and Asians are quick to support their American colleagues in criticizing them. It can indeed be counter-productive to attract more women and ethnic minorities on the basis of incorrect criteria, and their argument is that a problem does not solve itself by sheer weight of numbers. This is indeed a sad case, because many of those who are offered a job on the basis of these criteria are set up to fail.

There are good reasons to take this predominantly non-American criticism seriously. The main reason for the misconception is the erroneous type of universalism that often dominates the thought processes of many in the United States. At times equality is mistakenly taken for similarity: Michael Jackson seems to have a desire to turn paler every day and some women seem to find that the only way to survive is to take male behavior to heart. In the US there appears to be a strong belief in the effectiveness of making things similar in order to integrate them into a larger whole. The situation is very different in Europe and Asia. Often Americans tell us (informally) how "elegant" women in managerial positions are in Europe. They also remark that these women seem to choose other roles to their male counterparts in their uniform business suits. Where do you find more women in politics than in the Netherlands, for example?

Our 65,000 person intercultural database confirms a larger convergence over the last fifteen years in the responses of Americans, compared to European and Asians. Is this a typical case of non-American backwardness, or is there something deeper going on? North Americans have a typically Protestant urge to codify, standardize, and universalize; Asians and Europeans are more attracted to differences, diversity in the broadest sense of the word.

All this means is that there is a need for a diverse approach to the diversity issue. Obviously, there are universalities in the needs of minorities independent of the culture in which they try to give meaning to their lives, but the way to fulfil these needs is culturally determined. The dilemmas faced by minorities and those in power are the same, their resolutions are not. It does not matter whether you are American, Swedish, or Malaysian, if you are a woman and have a dilemma between economic productivity and childcare. Similarly, the need to have power and the lack of it is independent of culture. North Americans have a stronger inclination to choose a single horn of any dilemma when confronted with one and, in this way, they come up with universally applicable solutions. And they should do so. If you look at the American successes of engineering, MBA-driven companies, and the process of globalization, no one can doubt the strength of this approach. But we need another type of approach once we endeavor to globalize. Europeans and Asians have a greater need than Americans to create a dialogue between the groups and to resolve the dilemma beyond the level on which it occurs.

This scenario, as well as the success thereof, will depend on how those in charge take their responsibility. Europeans tend to have an advantage. They are more used to treating people equally rather than similarly. In this way, the more culturally sensitive US firms could also be better equipped to attain their goals elsewhere. This is the only way to eradicate an important false rationalization. There seems to be a great misunderstanding. Some Europeans and Asians claim that they do not have an "American Diversity" problem. I would argue that that is *not* the case. The whole world is facing similar challenges in this arena of diversity. It is the path toward reconciliation that needs to be redefined. I would suggest diversity in the approach to diversity. Only that can be the way to attain similar noble goals.

A CHALLENGE FOR THE MALE READER

Both Charles Hampden-Turner and I have burnt our fingers badly on the topic of political correctness in the USA. On one occasion when Charles was talking about the drama of American women in business, he made the following daring comment: "Did she get there through the bedroom or the boardroom?" The fierce reaction that followed was a clear sign that, as far as the average American was concerned, cynicism or any other form of high-contextual humor in this area was unacceptable. One participant from a large American company jumped up and took Charles's remark totally out of its carefully constructed context. This was the start of a great deal of trouble. Others fully understood the nature of the misunderstanding; however, Charles was no longer welcome. The company did not want to run the risk of being sued by an employee or the diversity council if Charles was to continue teaching. That was that.

A long time ago I also experienced a similar situation, when two female American participants were irritated because I introduced myself as forty-two, "though I look much older because I have three daughters." When the women walked out of the room I should not have said that they were lacking a sense of humor, as I too was told that I was no longer welcome.

I find it unthinkable that this happened to us, since we both appreciate women so much, especially because they possess many talents that monolithic men do not have. In a brilliant article, "The Structure of Entrapment," Charles Hampden-Turner described how the American diversity movement is heading in a dangerous direction. What do women, similar to many ethnic minorities, have to face? They are forced to gain their positions in a playing field where men make the rules. The higher a woman climbs the corporate ladder, the more she has to act like a man. Compared to her European and Asian female colleagues, she is forced to be more rule-driven, individualistic, rational, specific, achievement-oriented, and sequential.

It gets even worse. So-called "female" values like particularism, collectivism, emotional affect, a holistic approach, and synchronous thinking seem to be preserved in all cultures, except in the USA. American women score even lower on the aforementioned values than their male colleagues. How can this be? In order to survive in the predominantly male American business world women are forced to behave like men and have overcompensated. It is a game they can never win without doing so, because it has been designed by men. The Asian model does not seem to provide a solution either. In Asia women have often remained so subordinate that one finds hardly any occupying top positions.

Professor Nancy Adler of McGill University in Canada, together with us at Trompenaars Hampden-Turner, is looking for strong business reasons to show that women in the twenty-first century should fulfill top positions in organizations. Ross Ashby, the thermodynamicist, by his Law of Requisite Variety – which stipulates that every system will die if the variety of the system does not at least equalize the variety of its environment – provided our first argument. I believe we can significantly increase variety at the top, if we allow more women to reach these higher positions, especially now that internationalization provides us with more variation.

The second business argument concerns the mounting war for talent. Would there have been a war for talent, if companies had made more use of the available talent among women? The beauty of this talent is that it is fundamentally different from male talent. Perhaps a morphological metaphor is helpful in this regard. In *Sex and the Brain* by J. Durden-Smith it is shown that the highest brain activity in men takes place in either the right or the left half of the brain. Among women, however, the corpus callosum, the tissue which connects the two halves, seems to be the most active part.

How can we realize this business need? Unfortunately, we need the help of the ruling party. Therefore, I challenge male readers to facilitate this process, but not by making women behave more like men. I do not plead this cause because it is such a noble thing to do. Not at all! It is good business sense, and it adds sense to business.

OUR LADY IN ASIA

At present, most American and West European companies have made their core values or business principles more explicit. In the US one is already confronted by these in company lobbies.

At a typical East Coast firm I was struck by the fact that next to integrity, respect for other cultures stood high on the list of their core values. During our workshop we discussed an interesting case that had taken place in a pharmaceutical company in Turkey. Over the last ten years this company had managed to double its annual turnover. The licensee, now the director of the Turkish daughter company, was soon to retire. This came at a bad time as a new series of kidney dialysis products, which demanded a fundamentally different sales approach, was about to be launched on the market. The FDA (Food and Drug Administration) in the US had given their approval for these products two years previously. This endorsement was swiftly passed due to the outstanding help and work of Dr Betsy Cook who had been involved with the products from their inception. She was also due for promotion, and an appointment as head of a national activity was in line with her expectations. She would not only be able to raise the existing sales figures, but could also get the permission of the Turkish authorities. Despite all this, the Turkish management team had reservations about the arrival of Dr Cook. In Ankara she would be presiding over an established – and much older – management team, who had already done an excellent job in assisting the newly retired president. Although lacking the necessary experience with the new products they had, in the past, dealt with trickier situations.

You can already guess the nature of this dilemma. On the one hand,

we have an achievement-oriented American organization fully convinced that Dr Cook should be able to break through the glass
ceiling. With her impressive knowledge she would surely be able to
change the Turks' minds, especially with all that American experience to cash in on. On the other hand, Turkey is not known as the
most go-ahead culture as far as career possibilities for women are
concerned. Besides, the Turkish management team consisted mainly
of older men.

The discussion was stormy. The American majority of the workshop
participants thought that in a world moving towards globalization,
women should have every opportunity. The European and Asian
participants were unanimous that this example would not help the
cause of female co-workers in the future. The Turkish clients, and
the government, might well assume that the American company no
longer found the Turkish market interesting. The core values of the
company only made the dilemma more insurmountable.

In a similar manner, a Dutch–British company sent Rita de Vries to
Japan as delegation leader to negotiate the sale of a Japanese refinery. She was an experienced negotiator as well as being bright and
charming. After the Japanese had asked her when her boss would be
arriving, and her astonished retort that she and the three colleagues
reporting to her would be leading the negotiations, the Japanese
nodded in a friendly way and decided to postpone the negotiations
until after lunch.

The reaction of the Japanese only changed after they were informed
that de Vries was the most promising woman in the organization.
She was capable of making it to the top; her presence was not
intended to be insulting or to in any way diminish the business

interest of these transactions. After realizing this, the respect for the delegation leader grew. To come this far as a woman one had to be very good.

A certain logic has in the past helped Benazir Bhutto (Pakistan) and Tansu Çiller (Turkey) get to the top. The status that their fathers and their professorships gave them was of much more importance than the fact of them being women. We have seen this phenomenon more often with the placement of western personnel in countries that put more value on descent, age, and sex; for example young engineers sent to the Middle East to deal with large technical installations. Male/female is not the crucial issue here; it is rather one of (local) family, lineage, and age.

Americans tend to often choose a simplistic model: They send a variety of Americans to do a job for the locals. In contrast, Northern and Western European companies have always had more faith in trying to integrate the local population. But because the status of their young engineers was not sufficient to operate effectively in the Islamic world, they often created a dual hierarchy. The locals created the social hierarchy whereas the Europeans created the technical hierarchy. Naturally, this is costly.

Would this logic have been to Dr Cook's advantage? Of course it would. It is not only crucial that you respect other cultures but also that you respect your own egalitarian principles. The key to the reconciliation of this dilemma lies with the fact that status should be attributed to Dr Cook who would then be able to use her femininity to her advantage. For example, before the Turkish president retires, she should be allowed to work at his side for six months. His last assignment should have been to introduce her to clients, the government and the local management team as a very capable woman. In this way he could have afforded her status. One can see that integrity and respecting of other cultures at a higher level can indeed be united.

EUROVERGENCE

We are frequently asked whether the world of values is converging or diverging over time. If we reflect on political developments, we might conclude from the behavior of the Basques in Spain, the Catholics in Northern Ireland, the Albanians in Kosovo, or the Moluccans in Indonesia that cultures have an irresistible urge to diverge from each other.

While evaluating these relationships it is also appropriate to analyze European developments. In general, it appears that the cultures of Europe known in the Middle Ages were in fact much more similar than they are now. The process of the recent introduction of the euro seems to have caused a stimulus for some cultures to dig in even deeper. The British tend to emphasize even more loudly "we *and* the Europeans," as if they have never been part of Europe. Similarly, even the Dutch, one of the least Euro-sceptic nations, demonstrate ethnocentric behavior, and after a historic soccer match a Danish minister once said the words: "If you can't join them, beat them."

In my opinion, the European Summit at Nice in 2001 was at the very lowest level of European convergence. But what can you expect when the French are in the chair? The beginning of Chirac's first term as President several years ago symbolized the essence of French culture. He organized one nuclear test after another to show the world that France was still in charge. And when the world protested, he clearly demonstrated how bad his English was: he took the word "pro-test" literally and kept on testing.

Cultural anthropologists have fought a long intellectual battle over the question of whether the world was converging or diverging in its value systems. Perhaps the question has been wrongly posed. The evidence from our longitudinal research indicates that managers in countries like the Netherlands, USA, UK, and France, for which we have reliable data, have not changed significantly over the last twenty years. In contrast, Japanese managers seem to have changed dramatically, particularly towards individualism, but it also becomes apparent that variety by age and gender has decreased. Given our expectations and general observations of changes in society, it is not surprising that over the last few years, Japanese managers have drawn increasing attention to the role and contribution of successful women. The logical response of many Western women is that it was about time that they caught up with this trend.

What intrigues me now are the Central European cultures. These are occasionally described as "oscillating" cultures. Take Romania or Russia, for example. After the fall of the Wall they shifted to extreme individualistic orientations from extremely collectivistic values. This also led to pathological extremities that in turn stimulated collectivistic nostalgia. A Russian expatriate once indicated, out of envy for the richness of French grammar, that his language only needed three tenses: a nostalgic past, a bleak present, and an uncertain future. In the twenty years since we started our research at Trompenaars Hampden-Turner, we have found that almost all countries show a larger diversity within their boundaries (the multicultural society), except France and some parts of the UK.

If we analyze the broad spectrum of 65 countries represented in our cross-cultural database, then there is no single paradigm of converging or diverging values. The data reveal a very mixed pattern of different categories of tendencies. In Europe there is some degree of convergence, while in other regions and countries, people seem to re-emphasize their identity by pushing back from this shift to a more central tendency.

We need to emphasize that these inferences, and the debate presented thus far, are all based on mutually exclusive values: divergence and convergence. This does not take into consideration the so-called "principle of complementarity." Divergence and convergence, are they mutually exclusive? Not necessarily. If a culture wants to create wealth, a certain divergence of values will simultaneously demand a convergent system of orientations and vice versa. This is happening in Europe. Convergence there leads, for example, to an opposing separatism in the UK and Norway, or to Danish Euro-scepticism. You can observe the growth of a need for national identity as a response to cross-border influences.

What can business leaders learn from all this? As the environment continues to impose internationalization, we see similar effects. Within the Anglo-Saxon organization in particular, we can observe that the process of globalization has led to the need for convergence. Organizations in the USA and North-Western Europe have recently sought to introduce transparent and universal business principles and values. The response of the local operating companies has often been based on issues of local adaptation, as we have observed in the cases of GE, IBM, Cisco, Andersen, McKinsey, and Mars. Conversely, there are organizations that are driving for divergent values such as Unilever and KPMG. The former face the challenge of divergence in order to remain effective in their local environments. We might argue that in companies like McKinsey and Andersen, the first month of on-the-job training is aimed at how to fake listening to a client in order to be able to then try the universal tricks. Within KPMG, on the other hand, one listens so intensely to the client that the challenge lies in how to be able to actually serve them.

There is one principle we can all learn from this. You can only converge when you are diverse, or you can only diverge by starting from converging values. Healthy social systems have developed their own methods of achieving this. Some (as in the Netherlands) have first developed shared principles, in order to be able to frame and embrace departing values in a subsequent phase. Other social systems do this synchronously. They know where to converge in order to allow for divergence, just like a pendulum. This can move through a variety of values when it has a nail at the top from which it swings. Leadership is the rope that connects convergent and divergent values. The leader holding the rope knows very well that you can only diverge when you have something that also brings you back to convergence. Unfortunately, it seems that discussions in Europe too often oscillate between the need to make the nail as big as the pendulum, or to have a very heavy weight which seems to be held by much too thin a rope.

DIVERSITY IN BONDING: FROM EXCLUSIVE TO INCLUSIVE

One has become very aware of the after-effects of the terrorist attacks of September 11 in the USA. Business is recovering and is looking for new alternatives. It is quite striking that many North American organizations are now looking for programs that help them move beyond the stage of diversity. They seem to be looking for inclusion. After having devoted much attention to the issues pertaining to diversity they now seem to be focusing on what values are shared, what binds different populations and cultures together.

Let's look at the pendulum again. You can focus on the ball swinging in the diverse areas of life and values. But the pendulum is only effective when the nail in the top holds everything together. And the rope linking the nail to the ball, the shared to the diverse, is the essence of leadership. How to adapt global strategies locally or how to decentralize the central are key competencies of today's leaders. While diversity programs have taught us how to respect diverse cultures, inclusion will help people to know what we share. The way an organization reconciles inclusive values with diverse values is a measure of its maturity. And one of the main competencies underlying this maturity is the degree to which it can reconcile cultural differences. In this way my approach as described in earlier works (Hampden-Turner and Trompenaars, 2001) is very much in line with the thinking of Milton Bennett. He has developed the Developmental Model of Intercultural Sensitivity (DMIS) in which six phases of intercultural sensitivity are distinguished (see Bennett, 2001). The larger the sensitivity, the bigger the chance that the organization is taking advantage of cultural diversity.

The first three phases are *ethnocentric*. Here people unconsciously experience their own culture as "central to reality." The most basic form of ethnocentrism is best summarized in the first phase of *denial*. In this phase people are not yet able to see or experience cultural differences. There are no alternatives to their own logic, and if there are any they are seen as of less value or even inhumane. You can still find this attitude among managers in the Midwest of the US, for example, who will tell you "if we all just speak English everything will be OK." These people have never experienced a culture shock (and very likely will not), which is in great contrast to the people who surround them. They resolve cultural diversities by isolation or separation, as in the time of apartheid in South Africa. These managers have no clue about their own culture, because they lack any impetus which urges them to find out about themselves.

If we look at the following chart, we can see on the Y-axis "My values" and on the X-axis "Other Values." This first phase of denial can be put on the 1–1 position. These people and the organizations they represent don't know any other values and, therefore, lack any understanding of their own values. This type of organization is typically operates in one nation. The best they do, perhaps, is export goods to nations that they will never visit.

A second ethnocentric phase is the one of *defensiveness*. In this phase, people do experience cultural diversity; however the world is imme-

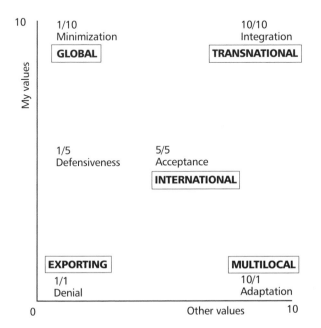

diately divided into "us" and "them," whereby "us" is – of course – superior to "them." This is typified by an internationalizing manager who is convinced that his organization (and the technology it represents) is the very best. Local differences are not really appreciated. If the threat of the defensive phase is being reduced by the assumption that, at the core, all persons are equal, one then enters the phase of *minimization*. This final level of ethnocentrism is approached in the so-called global organization, if we use the terminology used by Goshal and Bartlett (1998). One sees that cultural differences exist, and are tolerated, but a strong corporate culture, such as IBM in the past or GE, creates a strong pressure towards conformity. In the global organization there is a strong drive towards standardization. Management teams consist purely of nationals who have grown the business from home.

Bennet has characterized the first phase in *ethnorelativity* as the phase of *acceptance*. The managers of the organization have, through longstanding international contacts, understood that they have their own cultural context determining their behavior, and that other cultures give meaning to their lives in other ways. These organizations will pay serious attention to attracting staff from different and diverse cultures, and will fully understand the value of cultural diversity, far beyond the formal rule-based interpretation of diversity that we see so often. The top management of such an organization will, however, still typically consist of nationals from the country where headquarters are based, but there will be one or two exceptions. A good example of this *International Organization* (Ghoshal and Bartlett, 1998) is Walt Disney, which relates slightly to the countries – France and Japan – where it also have its theme parks. The last but one phase is referred to as *adaptation*. Managers are able to look through different lenses onto the world. They adapt easily to changing local circumstances. The Anglo-Dutch companies Royal Dutch Shell and Unilever (not by coincidence both bi-national organizations) are good examples of this group. And work gets done in the *Multi-National Organization.* Their managers are used to doing in Rome as the Romans do. Their organizations are easy to recognize, because they put a lot of effort into language training, and have many traditional cross-cultural training programs such as "doing business with the Japanese."

Transnational Organizations, of which probably Nokia and Applied Materials would be the best examples I know, have actually entered a sixth phase: that of complete *integration.* No one can do like the Romans anymore, since Rome no longer exists. When visiting Applied Materials, I learned that their top management of seven included seven different nationalities (even omitting the double nationalities), and that the organization was directed from different centers, of which several were outside the United States. Because all international activities are performed in multicultural teams, all managers are familiar with swapping from one cultural context to another. They view themselves as moving from one culture to the other, and do not perceive themselves as being at the center of the world. They very often use the interface between cultures as a platform from which to develop a hyperculture that transcends and makes use of the differences. Another example of this is Advanced Micro Devices and the way they operated in Dresden. In Chapter 3 I described how they beat Intel for the first time ever by combining the talents of German and US cultures with a disciplined program of dealing with diversity. Programs were developed to integrate and take advantage of the cultural differences, but around clearly defined business issues. Each culture tends to emphasize its uniqueness, and, therefore, is at least partially excluding other cultures.

However, the hyperculture of what Charles Hampden-Turner calls *reconciled values* is one that includes and brings together people with an individually exclusive identity. It is a corporate culture that brings people together around tensions between different viewpoints, and thereby time after time achieves advantages and benefits. It is also an organization that is explicit about its core values. Respect for diversity has become a "common good."

In our experience it is possible to help the growth towards the transnational organization in which values are reconciled into something that everyone shares. First of all attention needs to be given to the diversity of values that distinguishes one group from another. Once these diverse viewpoints are known, the process of respect needs to sink in. When differences are acknowledged and respected, it is time to integrate these values into a hyperculture of things shared.

CHAPTER 8

Corporate identity, culture and change

It is remarkable how often cultural background is ignored in both business and scientific discourse. It is necessary to consider why this is often ignored not only in alliances, but also in change management processes, in spite of the fact that it seems to be one of the major reasons for why such alliances and change processes fail.

Organizations are cultural constructs and, at the end of the day, any social system is a set of relationships between actors. The essence of these relationships is communication. Communication is the transport of information and information is the carrier of meaning. Since culture is the system of shared meaning, the organization is essentially a cultural construct.

WHY CULTURE MATTERS

I am still astonished at how often cultural backgrounds are neglected in business. I have previously discussed the reasons why so little attention is paid to the cultural factor in mergers and acquisitions. This is odd, really, as most of these alliances fall apart as a result. Another cause is the simplistic view about organizations that many managers and researchers have.

A little history lesson works wonders. Much research has been conducted into the area of employee efficiency at the end of the nineteenth and the beginning of the twentieth century. The beginning of the industrial revolution was marked by a need for increased productivity. A school of thought, best known as "Scientific Management," emerged in which people like Frederick Taylor and Henry Fayol occupied themselves with questions about efficiency. Taylor conducted many time and behavioral studies to determine how an employee could become more productive through a change in attitude and movement, and Fayol did good work on organizational issues such as how many subordinates an employer should ideally have and how many individuals should form a fully operational team. Although these approaches fitted well into considerations of the period, where productivity was seen as essential, they had their limitations. First of all, an employee was considered as a purely rational actor with specific (usually financial) motivations. The environment or context of the organization was set aside, which led to the conclusion that there was only one best way of organizing.

During the 1920s and 1930s there was a change which, interestingly, came about by accident. Researchers of the Scientific Management school studied the effects of light intensity on productivity in an assembly line factory in Hawthorne in the US. The intensity of light seemed to have a positive correlation with productivity. However, productivity also rose after reducing the intensity of light. It turned out that the attention that was given to the assembly line workers had more effect on their productivity than the intensity of the light. A new school of thought, the Human Relations school, developed under the influence of Elton Mayo and Fritz Roethlisberger.

Since then, much attention has been given to social aspects which play a role in the organization. The social actor was introduced but the organization remained a closed system. Simultaneously, a phenomenon developed which opened up the organization because extreme financing was needed. Management and property were divided; an organization was viewed as an open system. As the result of a study, better known as the "contingency theory," the end of the "one best way of organizing" approach was in sight. Statistical correlations between organizational structure and environmental circumstances were found. Structural aspects such as hierarchical layers and the average number of subordinates per employer were related to quantifiable contingency aspects. For example, technical complexity was expressed by R&D expenses pro capita, and complexity of the market as the average lifespan of a product. These context factors correlated significantly with structural characteristics. At the end of the 1970s the aspect of culture put in an appearance, but hardly seemed to affect anything mentioned earlier. This conclusion was summarized concisely in an article by David Hickson *et al.* entitled appropriately *The Culture-free Context of Organization Structure.*

Let us review this conclusion. While I was a researcher I walked through a Singaporean Shell refinery with its Dutch director. When I asked him in what way Singaporean culture had been integrated into his management he looked at me. In an attempt to understand the foolishness of my question he asked me if I was from Human Resources, and then replied by asking me "Did you really think I would give up the night shifts because the Singaporeans don't want to work during the night?" To continue – briefly – not only theory but also practice show us that technology and market were more important than a difficult aspect like culture.

What is lacking in this way of reasoning? Despite the fact that many organizations are open towards their environment and context, many of them still see an actor (or employee) as a limited person. In this approach, taken to the extreme, the actor and his perception continue to be neglected. The scientist sees himself reincarnated in the social scientist. The organization is observed through the eyes of the observer. What else can you do when looking at a molecule? In *Phenomenology of the Social World* Schutz gave a good example: the advantage of physics over the social sciences is that atoms and molecules don't talk back. The problem with human organizations is that humans produce reality. What does it matter what a researcher finds when the shared perception of humans is fundamentally different, considering that "what is defined as real is real in its consequences," as Schutz said?

When we look at the definition of structure we see that it is about a system of relationships among and between entities of the whole. The essence of these relationships is communication. And communication is the exchange of knowledge/information while knowledge/information is the carrier of meaning. That is why culture, as a system of shared meaning, is not an aspect that can easily be incorporated into analyses just like that. Culture is the context that dominates all relationships within the organization and its context, and it is time to start looking at the organization as a social construct. We can begin by engaging different types of consultants at McKinsey, BCG, and Accenture.

THE CULTURE OF CHANGE AND CHANGING CULTURE

It is striking how much the Anglo-Saxon model of change has dominated the world of change management. This is based on a task-oriented culture and the idea that traditions need to be forgotten as soon as possible. This seems to be fine in an Anglo-Saxon environment: you formulate a bunch of new goals, preferably in the context of a clear vision, you hire some consultants for a marginal US$300,000 a year (that figure excludes their bonus), and you dump the ones that do not believe in your clearly set goals. In this "Guided Missile" model the organization is conceived as a task-oriented instrument at the disposal of shareholders, where managers have an MBA and employees are called human resources.

The challenge lies in what to do when the surrounding culture is not aligned with this type of change logic. I remember an American manager from Eastman Kodak who had launched a very successful change program in Rochester, New York, and who cried on my shoulder after launching the formula in Europe. In great misery he said

> Fons, these French and Germans are unbelievably inflexible. I have done a whole round in Europe and in each of the countries many people seemed to support our vision. OK, the Germans had some problems with the process. They wanted to know all the procedural details and how these were connected to the change envisioned. The French were very worried about the unions. However we, as internal consultants and management, left with the idea that we agreed on the approach. When I returned some three months later to check how the implementation was going, I noticed that in France and Germany nothing had been started. Nothing!

Anyone with a bit of sensitivity to cross-cultural affairs could have predicted this. Germans often believe in vision, but without the proper structures, systems, and procedures that make this vision come alive, nothing will happen. Germans have a "push" culture: you push them in a certain direction. Compared to the North Americans they are not easily "pulled." You give them a goal or task and they follow, particularly when you pay them well to do it. In Latin and Asian countries management of change often means change the management. In their power-oriented, family ideology change will only happen when new points of departure are personalized. If "Monsieur le Président Directeur Général" does not fully back these points of departure, no pull or push will be effective.

This is one of the areas that creates dilemmas for Western organizations which, in their effort to globalize their activities, like to acquire and change foreign operations. Here's another example – an American organization thinks its Singaporean management takes too long to come to a decision. Consensus is nice, but doesn't serve in these times of great speed. The Singaporeans, for their part, think that the Americans take decisions too fast and without sufficient deliberation. They perceive that this will lead to major implementation problems, largely because too few people have been involved in the process.

On one extreme, you'll find that the desire of quick-on-their-feet managers often results in a "follow me, follow me," attitude causing a situation where – like lemmings – people all fall off a cliff together. At the other extreme you'll find the Asians who spend their time involving all ranks in order to gain consensus: the "Lost Democratic" model. Change is best directed towards the integration of both, guided by the Servant Leader. In this model you'll find that father figures, so popular in both Latin and Asian cultures, derive their authority from the way they serve their teams through their colleagues sharply formulated tasks.

How do you change the "Incubator" culture of an R&D laboratory, if your organization looks like the role-oriented culture of an "Eiffel Tower"? During my last job at Shell I often had dealings with sulking researchers who were failing to appreciate the HAY system of job evaluation. Firstly, they had to describe their job in great detail and then there was a panel that determined the number of points you could gather by adding the categories of Knowledge, Problem Solving, and Accountability. Finally, whether the incumbent actually performed that particular job had to be assessed. As the people responsible for this efficient, but rather ineffective, process we could only classify about five jobs a day. Moreover, the researchers often criticized the end result because their jobs had changed in the meanwhile: The job descriptions had been written some three months prior to the actual assessments. Can this rather static and rule- and procedure-driven instrument be applicable in a dynamic Incubator? Yes, it can – when we resolve some basic dilemmas.

On the one hand you have the swiftly changing environment of the R&D culture. On the other, there is the need for consistency between functions, both internationally as well as between divisions. We described the functions in a more abstract way, resulting in three types of researchers operating on three levels, and kept each description to one page only. In this way, we were able to summarize the jobs of some 1,200 staff in nine job descriptions. Points were allocated and the boss had to show that the job holder met all the criteria. This made the system less vulnerable to change. The strict management in London told us that this was to be considered an exception for R&D and that we should keep it to ourselves. It is interesting to see that five years later the whole of Shell took this benchmarking process as best practice and turned it into the new rule.

Management of change across cultures will be effective when one integrates opposing values on a higher level.

E-HYPE WITH VITAMIN R

In the good "old" economy you went to a car dealer, grabbed a few of the latest brochures in which were listed all the technical specifications for the model you were interested in, and settled into the leather seats of your new dream. The salesman, whom you knew from your previous purchase, would ask if everything was to your liking. The same applies to bookshops; my own preference is determined by the atmosphere of the shop and the quality of the advice given by the booksellers. For financial advisers, the same applies again. My preference is not so much related to the product or the service; it is more the quality of the financial institution and the people who work there, as is the case at Goldman Sachs, Merrill Lynch, MeesPierson, or Robeco. The personal and trusted relationship is the deciding factor for the ease with which I make a decision to invest in the innumerable soap bubbles that presently pass before me these days. E-trading on the Internet is therefore an appealing alternative choice. This kind of commerce based on good and value-free information is equally applicable to the acquisition of cars or books. Who needs a dealer? You click on a few screens and get the merchandise at a much lower price. End of the dealership, and long live the Internet. The new economy eats the old one – and at what a speed.

In consulting activities with Merrill Lynch and Goldman Sachs I have been involved in discussions on a similar theme. For example, despite the 17,000 brokers employed by Merrill Lynch in the US to give thoughtful advice within a personal relationship, discussions on e-hype were emotional. The new business created by Charles

Schwab had, by the launch of new internet services, captured 35 percent of the private banking market in one move. For a fraction of the price, results which were at least equal to those of more traditional approaches could be achieved. On the other hand, I heard the brokers plead for the continuation of the Merrill Lynch tradition, even saying that the personal relationship had to be deepened. Clients who would switch to the Internet regardless formed part of a category from which no one could earn a living: "We don't even want those clients in our portfolio." On the other hand, many threatened brokers shared the opinion that serious effort had to be undertaken to support Internet-based trading of shares with the powerful research database of the organization: "Wake up, the new economy has already got out of bed." As a result of these differing opinions Merrill Lynch ran the risk of going for a little bit of Internet, or even worse, of splitting the traditional innovative services into two separate businesses, thereby creating strong internal competition.

Many enterprises are struggling these days with this dilemma between old and new economic orientations. Oscillating between the two is deadly. We can see a new business model emerging in successful companies, integrating the strength of the individual relationships in their existing dealer networks with the power of e-commerce. In essence, it focuses on the ease with which a client can collect value-free information thanks to the relationship with the dealer and other users. The launch of this new business model, among others, by Merrill Lynch in the fall of 1999 has generated solid results for the company, and the market share lost to Charles Schwab has been regained by luring back former clients. Despite that, Wall Street analysts were not impressed because it did not result in a new category of client. What it does show, however, is that by uniting old and new economic values one can deliver more services to existing customers.

A few experiments at Merrill Lynch have generated interesting insights. Brokers there have coached their clients on the Internet; training courses were offered to these clients to enable them to use the internet effectively. In addition, they could get in touch with their personal brokers through the internet. Webcams were even installed for some clients, to allow direct interaction with their brokers. The final result was that private investors said they had never before enjoyed such a good relationship, and the brokers reported that it was more fun to work with clients who were better informed.

I can already visualize it. I see my dream car on the internet after a few clicks. I can change the colour and make spoke hubcaps appear on the screen. I can assess the interior look. That will result in my spending less time with my dealer on trivial details, but I will go round to him anyway to test the seats and for the annual service.

For enterprises, the success of the new economy will partly depend on how new features are integrated with the power of the old economy. E-hype will make us even more dependant on vitamin R – R for relationships.

SCENARIO PLANNING: CAN THE FROG JUMP?

Of course you know how to prepare frogs. When you throw frogs into a pan of boiling water, they will immediately jump out, so what do you do? You take a bowl of lukewarm water and throw some frogs in, then let the water temperature rise very slowly until it reaches boiling point. The frogs will not notice and will soon be ready for lunch. That was not the problem Shell had, according to people who knew Shell. The problem was that Shell's frogs could not jump – the company was not able to react quickly to a major change in its environment, such as an oil crisis.

In the beginning of the 1970s, with help of this story, you could get Shell employees involved in scenario exercises. Scenario planning came to maturity at Shell's Group Planning in the beginning of the 1970s under the inspiring leadership of Pierre Wack. He defined scenario planning as "a discipline for rediscovering the original entrepreneurial power of creative foreseeing in contexts of accelerating change, complexity and uncertainty."[8]

A lot of misunderstandings arose around the use of this discipline, mostly because it was too often used as a trick offering a swift solution. It is anything but that. My experience with handling this methodology gives me a similar feeling to the handling of methods of multicultural consulting work. Scenario planning also needs to be integrated into the day-to-day business of the organization and not seen as a side issue that is finished with after a two-day workshop.

What is scenario planning *not*? Scenario planning is not a special version of contingency planning, or "what if?" planning. It is not a method of improving the quality of forecasting, either. In essence, scenario planning originated from the philosophy that the forecasting of a univocal environment becomes more useless with every passing day, not only because of the increasingly turbulent world, but also because of the interesting thought that forecasting can itself influence the environment.

The best way to find out how state-of-the-art of scenario planning works is to join one of the World View meetings of the Global Business Network. This organization was set-up by Shell trainees Peter Schwartz, Napier Collyns, Jaap Leemhuis, and Kees van der Heijden, some of those who control the essence of this method its and processes.

Now, what *is* scenario planning? In essence, the outcome of a scenario planning process is an organizational culture in which employees are able to act more quickly in different environments. Usually, at first, existing research is consulted on relevant trends in social, economical, political, technological, and ecological environments, and core players are interviewed inside and outside the relevant organizations. To this end, GBN often consults its network of "Remarkable People," scientists and artists, varying from musician Brian Eno to anthropologist Katherine Bateson. After this initial step the management, under the leadership of highly qualified GBN facilitators, undergoes a process from which two to four descriptions of the future emanate, all internally logical and highly possible.

The next step concerns the preparation of the organization of each scenario. This is where the method of reconciling dilemmas developed by my organization is of particular help. Those who prepare themselves for different scenarios will often be confronted with conflicting aspects; scenarios are instruments for arranging perceptions of alternative futures. Often scenarios are a couple of stories, written or orally expressed, built around a number of specifically chosen plots. Stories organize knowledge and bring a set of points of view, both quantitative and qualitative, to the surface.

In this way decision makers are informed of a wealth of opportunities, opportunities they could never have imagined, in spite of their undoubtedly high intelligence. Good scenarios often break with stereotypes, and can be seen as exercises for the future. However, they do not give a more accurate view of the future but rather the possibility of starting an effective strategic conversation with employees and stakeholders outside the organization. And that is somewhat different from choosing the most probable future scenario.

In my opinion, the effectiveness of this method highly is highly dependent on the supervisors of the process. Without a doubt, GBN is the world leader in this area, because all the processes of this method are implemented. In addition, in the last fifteen years they have gathered together an impressive network of clients, who are offered a wide scale of services for an annual fee. The most important part of this is the exchange of mutual experiences during World View meetings. The combination of master classes, where internal people are trained, with a network of Remarkable People, make GBN an unbeatable group.

The method of scenario planning is particularly suited for those organizations which have troubles with measuring the temperature of the water in which their frogs are swimming (old economies) and those organizations with frogs that do not have a clue in which direction to jump while the water is boiling (new economies). Furthermore, this method helps to link them together.

THE VALUE OF CORE VALUES

Recently, we removed a sign that was hanging above the front door of our house. It read: "We don't kill people here."

Strangely enough, many guests had become somewhat agitated by this announcement, while we consider it a very important value in our family. Apparently, the impact on our visitors was similar to the irritation I feel when entering an American company and being greeted by king-size posters declaring "Integrity." Why do I feel such irritation?

That is simple. Because it indicates that, seemingly, integrity is not part of the normal pattern of that organization. All the core values of an organization are values that have not yet become norms. To clarify: a norm is a common orientation of a group of individuals towards that which one should do. On the other hand a value is a common orientation toward that which one would like to do. In a successful culture, people tend to consider what should be done as also being desirable. When that happens, those values have become norms, and they will become basic assumptions at the core of the culture concerned.

Such assumptions are almost never included in a list of organizational principles. Often, these norm values are part of the guts of an organization. Does that mean that they have no significance? On the contrary, their most important role is that they make things open to discussion.

We are often asked whether an international or multi-divisional organization can actually formulate core values. The source for that question is whether, because of national or corporate cultural differences, what one part may consider desirable, another might see as unwanted or even offensive.

However, core values should not be diluted into a number of bland and abstract statements, with which everyone can agree. A good test for the introduction of core values is to check whether they lead to a dilemma between that core value and the value of the business unit or division. Within such a tension, an organization and its units can create an identity.

From time to time in my professional practice I receive assignments that are very special because one learns so much from them. Two years ago, a Dutch organization – CSM – asked Trompenaars Hampden-Turner to help them define their core values, and make them work in real life. We were invited to facilitate the development process of their values at their annual management meeting with their five divisions. Because of strong growth through acquisitions in Finland, the United States, and Europe, the whole organization was looking for a renewed identity. In addition, the company had difficulty explaining to financial analysts what it stood for.

After a few creative sessions, with a very impressive team, four values emerged: Continuous Improvement, Openness, Stakeholder Value, and Entrepreneurship. But that was not the end of it. The CEO and his managers wanted to drive these values into the daily practice of the five divisions.

When introducing core values, tensions with current reality always emerge. The top 30–100 people from each division worked on these tensions for two days. One of these groups, in a division consisting primarily of previously family-owned enterprises, had no problem whatsoever with the value of Openness. However, between the ex-family businesses, the openness was almost non-existent, as they did not know each other well enough. The resulting "required action plan" was then easily defined by using this cultural value of openness between the different businesses.

In contrast, in another division, which had already operated for decades in a reasonably protected national environment, entrepreneurship was watered down to intrapreneurship, and generally not well regarded. There, the action plan was to identify opportunities to stimulate the internally oriented employees to use their talents on the outside. One division actually reformulated some core values to make them more applicable to their environment. The discussion revealed that, in reality, the Continuous Improvement value meant that the client was not always on the center stage when the alternative was to invest in better manufacturing techniques. The required reconciliation which emerged was "Through the continuous improvement of knowledge about our clients, we will satisfy their changing needs with our superior products."

Apparently contradictory values can, through this process, be reunited or reconciled at a higher level. One could state that value is not being added by leaders, because only simple values add up. It is the leader's vision, and the teamwork at the top of the organization, that create the open space for their people to work on these tensions and dilemmas. And core values are not just taken for granted.

ENGLISH CORE VALUES: BACK TO BASICS

It has been turbulent in the UK. Some of its own people have been criticizing ex-Prime Minister John Major because of his affair with ex-Health Minister Edwina Currie. Is that so bad? No, but he shouldn't have given a "back to basics" speech asking the British public to return to traditional family values if he wasn't prepared to do that himself. Yes, the British started to discuss their core values some twenty years ago. But what are the traditional values of the British, or rather of the English?

This is a particularly interesting topic in view of the recent publication by the UN Committee on the Rights of Children. Great Britain was lambasted for its cruel approach to disobedient children both by their parents and in school; it almost seemed that slaps in the face and a few well-directed kicks were the rule rather the than exception. And the report also refers to the large number of young people currently in British jails. In addition, there is mention of appalling poverty among youngsters (especially students) and the high numbers of teenage pregnancies. Is this reflected in the fact that the British have a National Society for the Prevention of Cruelty to Children but a Royal Society for the Protection of Animals?

In addition, the 2001 national census in the UK showed that at least 600,000 young men aged 20–30 years old have flown the UK to seek happiness elsewhere. The social scientists have difficulties in accounting for this statistical black hole. It is certainly not true, I hope, that they are leaving to avoid jail, poverty, or responsibility for their part in the teenage pregnancies!

No, say my British colleagues in our office at Trompenaars Hampden-Turner. It is just a modern expression of the "Grand Tour" that once enabled young British men to go beyond their island mentality for a while. In the eighteenth and nineteenth centuries many upper-class British males in their twenties went for a cultural tour through Venice, Paris, and Berlin in order to enlarge their horizons. For women, the equivalent was "Coming Out," the "Season" in which girls were introduced to society – and to suitable male counterparts. These were ways for islanders to spread their wings. Not much has changed; it is just being manifested in new ways.

So what are the most striking values of the English? At first they seem as much obsessed by rules as their closest friends, the North Americans. Our cultural database of 6,000 English and 5,000 Americans also indicates this high degree of universalism. However, there is a significant difference between these Anglo-Saxon cultures. The Americans have an enormous need to codify their laws which is also revealed by them being the first nation to have a written constitution. In contrast, the English prefer rules to be implicit, respected by gentlemen. English law is based on jurisprudence accumulated case by case. The English, along with the Americans, have also developed a rather strong individualism and internal control. It is not for nothing that "I" is written with a capital letter and that relatively little discussion is needed on how the Iraqis need to be tackled.

The "stiff upper lip" is typically English. A real "gentleman" is not allowed to show any emotions, even though they have them, the same as other people. I frequently ask my English guests how they reveal their emotions, and the answer equally frequently lies in the direction of humor. In this particular area there is also a great difference from the Americans, whose humor usually has few nuances and embraces exaggeration. The high-contextual humour of the English is subtly imbued with cynicism; a splendidly diplomatic manner for anyone who wants to express their emotions. This has been an important element in the success of Unilever and Shell. As I've said before, there the jokes come from the English and the Dutch laugh. I have also mentioned the diffuse nature that reveals itself in aloofness and indirect communication. Someone who is Dutch or American will cut you dead if they don't like you, but an English person may stab you in the back without you even noticing: "You have an interesting personality," for example, usually means exactly the opposite.

Finally there is the paradox of how power is legitimatized. On the one hand, business performance is much appreciated and helps individuals receive rapid promotion. On the other hand, it is still relatively difficult to move from the working class to the levels of the more genteel.

These may be simplifications, but I have tried to avoid any overly critical note, especially as the English are very well able to delineate – and comment on – the restrictions of their own culture. They would never allow the continental Europeans to do this for them; people over there lack the spirit and humour to do that. In this way fog still looms in the Channel and North Sea.

THE CULTURE OF MERGERS

As we have seen, a lot of research has been done into the causes for failure in mergers and acquisitions. Consulting firms have published endless lists of deficiencies. Their conclusions point in the same direction: top talent leaving the organization, a lowered collective and individual productivity, incomplete or inadequate communication, the wrong positioning of key managers; not enough "hands on" management including attention to genuine problems on the shop floor, lack of clear direction during the integration and implementation process, and insensitivity to expectations from the business.

All these consultants point to the influence of differences between corporate and national cultures, although they disagree on the order of importance.

I do not think it is good practice to list culture as one of the many factors. Culture is the context against which *all* of the specific factors should be considered in order to create an effective integration process. I'll illustrate this briefly with a few examples from the Netherlands.

First of all, the thesis that large organizations are swallowing smaller ones, and that the aggressive successfully dominate the meek does not hold true. In the Dutch environment, the acquiring party's characteristic was one of dedication to its own core values and of further enlargement through the acquisition. This received much more emphasis than purely financial targets. This could be seen, for example, with the retailer Ahold taking over the Stop & Shop formula from KKR, which established its reputation as a wholesale buyer of retail businesses. KKR had made the unit lean and mean and very profitable without, however, paying a lot of attention to the level of motivation within the organization. Ahold focused particularly on this point and may even improve results further.

In successful acquisitions, you tend to learn more from listening to and understanding the acquired party rather than imposing your values, systems, and procedures on them. The case of Akzo Nobel, the Dutch–Swedish chemical and pharmaceutical company, stresses the importance of bringing together different points of view in order to spread best practices that might even result in adopting the IT systems of the acquired party, as Buhrmann did with Corporate Express. Another significant factor was that the takeover "objects" often made their own choice between potential acquirers based on perceived cultural fit. We have seen few hostile bids.

A common thread running through almost all the cases was that the success of the alliance was dependant on the level of personal trust and deep attachment between the leaders of both organizations. An excellent example of this can be found in the acquisition of the Belgian bank BBL by the Dutch ING, which positioned its key people on the board in low-profile positions to gradually allow for the gaining of confidence.

It is evident that not all cultures easily meld, and that a marriage cannot be forced without a huge price sometimes being paid. Akzo finally found Nobel after the mismatch with Courtaulds. The British command-and-control corporate culture did not combine well with Akzo's consensus oriented management style, with which the Swedes were more at ease.

On the contrary, successful acquisition processes typically seek dialogue and complimentarity. This is often the opposite of "one size fits all." The new culture results from value synergies and respect for the others' values.

Leadership continuity is also a positive integration factor, especially when other management levels are invited and involved in the integration process as equal contributors for their areas of competence. This is reinforced if achievement is recognized and credited, irrespective of the original background. A consequence of this attitude may be that less competent managers will ultimately leave, thus creating room for talent.

It may be that Dutch organizations are more effective in creating and achieving synergy than organizations of larger, more dominant countries. In *The Seven Cultures of Captialism* Charles Hampden-Turner has stated that the Dutch talent for dealing with cultural differences, paradoxes, and dilemmas could support this statement.

The uniquely Dutch way of dealing with acquisition may ultimately be to pursue both social and financial goals. Paying attention to social aspects pays off in the end.

Dilemmas to be addressed in globalizing organizations

I have previously stated that university educations and too much in-company training are still based on Cartesian logic and scientific method, where problems are considered solvable because they are framed as closed systems. Cultures were seen as static points, positioned on dual axis maps, where one cultural category excludes the other. In this system of logic, established analytical procedures are culture neutral and value-free. Cultures are linear with more or less of a fixed quantity. Based on this thinking we can interpret cultural differences as positions of relative salience on a limited set of variables or dimensions.

But globalizing organizations are stifled by this approach because, among other things, it doesn't answer the "so what?" and "where should we go from here?" questions. As I said earlier, another approach is needed in which culture dances from one preferred end to its opposite and back. As such, value dimensions self-organize in systems to generate meaning. As a consequence, I can therefore define four convictions relevant to the future of globalizing organizations:

1. Knowledge and understanding is stored within corporate cultures, and, most especially, in the relationships between people.

2. "Strategy" consists not of one infallible master plan or grand strategy but of hundreds of trials and tentative initiatives. As Lord John Browne, CEO of BP Amoco, recently said "Giving up the illusion that you can predict the future is a very liberating moment. All you can do is to give yourself the capacity to respond…The creation of this capacity is the purpose of strategy."

3. Learning occurs when we eliminate the less successful trials and intensify and explore the more successful ones by continuously monitoring feedback from activities. An unending inquiry into what helps customers and pays us is successful insurance.

4. Management of change is based on "adding value" rather than simply discarding the values of the old situation.

At Trompenaars Hampden-Turner our approach to understanding a corporation has been to investigate its dilemmas. The word "dilemma" comes from the Greek meaning "two propositions." Based on the evidence from our research, all cultures and corporations have developed habitual ways of resolving dilemmas. For example, corporations are both well centralized and highly decentralized at the same time; the success of a company will depend, among other things, both on the autonomy of its parts and how well the information arising from this autonomy has been centralized and coordinated.

In the last couple of years our organization has progressed from simply trying to help clients to become aware of cultural differences by mapping those differences on profile scales. We have also charted the dilemmas that arise when you respect the differences between cultures and their value-orientations. So what are the main dilemmas for leaders in globalizing organizations?

The principal cluster is a category concerned with dilemmas around issues in leadership, such as cost versus investment; short term versus long term; internal organization focus versus external focus on environment, and finally leadership versus management.

The second main category arises in the area of integration of values. They range from core values versus local values, centralization of systems versus decentralization of processes, shareholder value versus stakeholder value, through to the integration of businesses versus the differentiation of businesses.

The increasing internationalization of business has caused many functional disciplines to redefine and rethink their very essence. A third main cluster of dilemmas are centered in the area of functional dilemmas. The most prominent are between functions such as R&D and Marketing. In the areas of marketing we found that dilemmas of global versus local, clients and branding, and specific service culture versus holistic integration of service culture were common.

There were, as expected, extensive dilemmas in HR, notably centralization of HR systems versus decentralization of HR processes, and implicit or tacit versus explicit or codified knowledge. There are also the problems of teamwork and loyalty to management decisions versus expression of personal dissenting convictions; development as professional versus development as generalist; task orientation versus people orientation; entrepreneurship versus control/account-ability, and mentoring versus managing.

Another cluster lies in the area of globalization in which the follow-ing frequently occur: face-to-face management versus remote management; business unit versus shared responsibilities in a matrix, and one definition of integrity worldwide versus local inter-pretations.

In the area of diversity we find yet another cluster: similarity of gen-der versus different roles; diversity of values versus inclusion, and convergence versus divergence.

At the nomothetic level, there are important dilemmas around cor-porate identity, culture and change. Examples include change versus constancy; one identity through core values versus many identities for intimacy of operations; bottom-up values versus top-down, and values in use versus espoused values. Framing these as dilemmas enables us to elicit their associated tensions and thereby find a starting point for reconciliation .

The stories and metaphors in this book show clearly that globalizing organizations need to face a fundamental choice in approaching these new type of realities. Some companies go into complexity reduction mode by building more and more systems and control mechanisms, while others recognize the paradoxes and build them into complexity absorption – they just live with it, and recognize that it happens. The latter are at an enormous advantage, because they include the former and take things to a higher level.

References

Ackoff, R. (1987) *The Art of Problem Solving Accompanied by Ackoff's Fables*. New York: Wiley.

Adler, N. J. and Izraeli, D. N. (1994) *Competitive Frontiers: Woman Managers in a Global Economy*. Oxford: Blackwell.

Belbin, M. R. (1981) *Team Roles at Work*. London: Butterworth-Heinemann.

Bennis, W. (1994) *On Becoming A Leader*. Cambridge, MA: Perseus.

Bouchiki, H. and Kimberly, J. (2000) Management 21C: new visions for the new millennium. In S. Chowdhury (ed.), *Management 21C: Someday We'll All Manage This Way*. London: Financial Times Management

Bouchiki, H. and Kimberly, J. (2001) All change in the customised workplace in mastering people management, *Financial Times*, 22 October.

Carlzon, J. (1989) *Moments of Truth*. London: HarperCollins.

Clark, S. C. (2000) Work/family border theory: a new theory of work/family balance. *Human Relations*, June.

Durden-Smith, J. (1983) *Sex and the Brain*. Westminster, MD: Arbor House.

Hall, E. T. (1973) *The Silent Language*. New York: Anchor.

Hampden-Turner, C (1995/6) *The Structure of Entrapment*. The Deeper News, Global Business Network (www.gbn.com).

Hampden-Turner, C. and Trompenaars, F. (1993) *The Seven Cultures of Capitalism*. New York, Doubleday.

Hampden-Turner, C. and Trompenaars, F. (1997) Response to Geert Hofstede. *International Journal of Intercultural Relations*, 21(1), 149–159.

Hampden-Turner, C. and Trompenaars, F. (2001) *Building Cross-cultural Competence*. New Haven and London:Yale University Press.

Hickson, D. J., Hinings, C. R., McMillan, C. J. and Schwitter, J. P. (1974) The culture-free context of organization structure: a tri-national comparison. *Sociology*, 8, 49–80.

Hofstede, G. (1996) Riding the waves of commerce: a test of Trompenaars' 'model' of national cultural differences. *International Journal of Intercultural Relations*, 20(2), 189–198.

Kaplan, R. S. and Norton, D. P. (1996) *The Balanced Scorecard: Translating Strategy into Action*. Cambridge, MA: Harvard Business School Press.

Kolb, D. A (1983) *Experiential Learning: Experience as the Source of Learning and Development*. Engelwood Cliffs, NJ: Prentice Hall.

Kotter, J. P (1999) *What Leaders Really Do*. Cambridge, MA: Harvard Business School Press.

Kouzes, J. M. and Posner, B. Z. (2002) *The Leadership Challenge*, 2rd edn. San Francisco: Jossey-Bass.

Laurent, A. (1977) *Why the Matrix Organization Failed in France*. INSEAD Working Paper, Fontainbleau.

Leach, P. (1994) *Family Businesses*, 2nd edn. London: Kogan Page.

Marcuse, H. (1964) *One Dimensional Man*. Boston, MA: Beacon Press.

Mark, M. and Pearson, C. S. (2001) *The Hero and the Outlaw, Building Extraordinary Brands through the Power of Archetypes*. New York: McGraw-Hill.

Morgan, J. (1991) *Cracking the Japanese Market*. New York: The Free Press.

Nonaka, I. and Takeuchi, H. (1995) *The Knowledge-creating Company: How Japanese Companies Create the Dynamics of Innovation*. Oxford: Oxford University Press.

Ockrent, C. and Séréni, J. P. (1998) *Les Grands Patrons. Comment ils voient notre avenir* Paris: Plon.

Parsons, T. (1952) *The Social System*. London: Routledge.

Porter, M. E. (1998) *The Competitive Advantage of Nations: With a New Introduction*, 2nd edn. New York: The Free Press.

Rapaille, G. C. (2001) *7 Secrets of Marketing in a Multicultural world*. Provo, UT: Executive Excellence Publishing.

Schein, E. (1991) *Organizational Culture and Leadership*. San Francisco: Jossey-Bass.

Schutz, A. (1967) *Phenomenology of the Social World*. Evanston, IL: Northwestern University Press.

Swaffin-Smith, C., Woolliams, P. and Tomenko, H. (2000) *Towards a Unified Model for Small to Medium Enterprise Business Paradigms*. London: Earlybrave.

Trompenaars, F and Hampden-Turner, C. (1997) *Riding the Waves of Culture: Understanding Diversity in Global Business*, 2nd edn. New York: McGraw-Hill.

Trompenaars, F. and Hampden-Turner, C. (2001) *21 Leaders for the 21st Century*. Oxford: Capstone.

Ulrich, D. and Lake, D. (1990) *Organizational Capability*. New York:Wiley.

Wack, P. (1984) http://www.gbn.com/public/gbnstory/scenarios/.

Index